JAMAICA AIRMAN

JAMAICA AIRMAN

A black airman in Britain
1943 and after

by
E. Martin Noble

London : Port of Spain

First published in 1984 by New Beacon Books Ltd., 76 Stroud Green
Road, London N4 3EN, England.

© 1984, E. M. Noble

ISBN 0901241 58 X hardback
    0901241 59 8 paperback

Printed by Villiers Publications Ltd., Ingestre Road, London NW5
1UL, England.

Dedication

I wish to dedicate this book to my two daughters Valerie and Denise, and all West Indians in Britain in recognition of their struggle to survive against prejudice and injustice.

Acknowledgement is here made to Encyclopaedia Britannica and the Jamaica High Commission Office, London, for historical background material, and the Royal Automobile Club of Britain for the historical information on my French holiday tour.

CONTENTS

Preface . . . . p. 5
Chapter 1. *Childhood* 7
Chapter 2. *Life in the Big City* 17
Chapter 3. *En Route to the War & Training*
     in Yorkshire 31
Chapter 4. *Loving in Cornwall & First*
     Footing in Scotland 44
Chapter 5. *A Fight in Manchester* 59
Chapter 6. *Return to the Air Force* 70
Chapter 7. *Tour of France 1951* 83
Chapter 8. *Back to Civvy Street* 97

PREFACE

As I stood on the deck of the trim cargo vessel, in which I was one of a small number of passengers, and surveyed the scene nature was unfolding to my critical gaze, a warm glow pervaded the atmosphere; the forerunner of shimmering tropical heat tempered by cooling sea breezes. The sun, that now golden sphere, just barely visible as it rose slowly from behind Warieka Hills dispersing the early morning mist in its path.

Warieka Hills, 'dear old Warieka Hills', standing sentinel to the east of the city of Kingston, Jamaica, bidding farewell to the departing traveller and beckoning a welcome to her returning exiled sons. To the south west lay the small island of Lyme Quay, to which as a young man in my late teens, I made many a fishing trip — usually after an overnight stay at Fort George, Port Royal, the former headquarters of the notorious pirate Captain Morgan.

From my present position Port Royal was clearly visible as a collection of moored craft and harbour buildings, with a background of dark foliage rising beyond the immediate expanse of water.

For a brief while I allowed my mind to wander back to its historic past. I tried to conjure up a picture in my mind's eye of the young naval commander, Horatio Nelson, provisioning and re-fuelling his fleet in readiness to do battle with the French; of Morgan and his crew of cut-throats, wining and womanising after a successful raid on some unfortunate Spanish merchant-man or galleon. Today it beggars the imagination to think that one of the most wanted criminals of the day was, when expediency demanded, made Governor of the British Colony of Jamaica, and, as if to add insult to injury, in later British history is foisted on an unsuspecting reading public as a hero and man of honour.

History records that Port Royal was at that time the richest and wickedest spot on earth. A far cry from the broken-down and destitute island harbour it now is, with its deserted and decaying fort, and its inhabitants eeking out a bare existence as

5

fishing folk, or working on the coaling station which was at this time still maintained by the British navy.

The second world war brought prosperity of a sort to these shores. Apart from the increased number of ships that used the port for re-fuelling, there was the recently constructed air base at Pallisadoes. The building of the Pallisadoes base, together with the service road linking it to the port of Kingston, provided work for both the peoples of Port Royal and the mainland. This relief however was short lived, and many of Jamaica's sons, either from patriotic feelings or sheer economic necessity (and I suspect more from the latter than the former), enlisted in the armed forces of the Crown. In the former category, naïvely, was myself.

At my previous on-deck viewing I had watched a receding landscape with mixed feelings; wondering what the future held in store for me as I sailed away from my beloved island home, bound for England to serve as a member of the Royal Air Force. Now after more than twenty adventure packed years, I was again viewing the same scene. This time as a returning exile, if only on holiday, but with the same mixed feelings. What had the future in store this time? Would I be welcomed as a war hero, or jealously resented for my modest success and survival? The only thing I could be absolutely certain of at that precise moment, was that my dear old Mamma would be at the quayside, dressed in her 'Sunday best' to welcome me. My darling Grandma (Moma) had already passed away these thirteen years.

The sound of my name brought me back from my reverie. It was a fellow passenger, a Jamaican widow returning to the island after the death of her husband whilst serving in Germany with the British Army of the Rhine. 'It is time you were getting your luggage together,' she was saying.

CHAPTER I. *Childhood.*

This is the story of my life as an airman, and the rejection I met as a civilian once the war was over. And like all good stories, it begins with my childhood.

I was born in Kingston, Jamaica, in the year 1917. The fact that I was born in Kingston was purely accidental as my parents lived in St Ann's Bay, in the parish of St Ann, which is on the north west coast of the island. As I understand it, my mother was visiting an aunt of hers, and making last minute purchases for my impending birth. The happy event was not expected for many weeks yet, but after a strenuous day's shopping, Mamma, on returning home, retired to her room with severe tummy pains. The doctor was called, and he immediately rushed the patient off to the nearby maternity hospital, where some hours later I had my first glimpse of the world. A world which was only just recovering from its latest mad holocaust. As soon as the premature baby was strong enough to travel, Mamma returned to her own home in St Ann's Bay.

My early years were typical of the children of most middle class Jamaican families of the period. I should perhaps mention here that I never knew my father who had emigrated to the USA. My mother and I lived with my grandparents who had three daughters, my mother being the eldest. Being the first grandchild, and a boy at that, my grandparents virtually took me over and treated me as the son they longed for but never had. Grandpa Walters died whilst I was still a very small boy. In fact all I can remember of it is that he was laid out in the room he and Grandma had shared, and a lot of people came to look at him, and there was crying and a lot of eating and drinking. After Grandpa's death Mamma went to live and work in Port Maria a town about 27 miles to the east of St Ann's Bay, and on the north of the island. From then on Grandma Walters (or as I came to call her 'Moma') became my mother for all practical purposes.

Our home was comfortably furnished and consisted of three bedrooms, a spacious dining-room, a guest room, a small nursery and a large parlour. Moma had the largest bedroom in order to accommodate her over-sized four-poster bed. The four-poster is particularly remembered and well loved because beneath its ample proportions I was on many occasions to escape the wrath of Mamma or Moma, and a justly deserved spanking.

In the parlour was a victrola gramophone with an enormous horn, a wickerwork settee, and cane seated chairs. On the verandah hung pots of flowers suspended by wires. There was a small flower garden in the front and to the left of the house. There was also, at the back, a small outhouse occupied by two resident maids. A few banana trees and one solitary coconut tree. As soon as I could walk I tried to climb the coconut tree. It was, however, several years, many falls, and numerous cuts and bruises later before that feat was ever accomplished.

One of the highlights of my early boyhood was the occasions when I would be sent to Lyons, the wholesale grocers in the town, with an order for goods to restock the grocery shop which Moma ran. Although I was not expected to wait for their despatch, I nevertheless invariably did so. If the order was a large one it would be despatched by motor truck, and I would travel back alongside the driver in the cab. If on the other hand it was a small order, it would be sent by 'mule dray', and I would travel back perched atop bags of sugar, rice or flour, or, more uncomfortably, on cases of condensed milk. Apart from the hard cases I much preferred this mode of travel to the cab of a truck.

The family at this time consisted of Moma, Mamma, Aunt Norah and Aunt May. Aunt Norah, who worked at Dawkins Drapery Store in town, was a hypochondriac. Her room, which she shared with Aunt May, was like a chemist's shop with medicine bottles and pill boxes. Her aches and pains were the standing family joke. Aunt May, who was 17 years old and out of school, took music lessons from the minister's wife at the Manse, where she also spent the last two years of her schooling.

The Church of England minister and his wife, who were from England, ran the most exclusive girls' school in the parish. I think their name was Thornton, and they had a son of about my own age called Basil. Aunt May and myself were great friends, but my special favourite was Moma who literally spoilt me. Before Mamma left home for Port Maria, Moma would often say to her: 'Adlin (that's my mother's name), leave the boy alone, he is only a baby, and a healthy one at that. The time for you to really start worrying is when he is quiet and gives no trouble, by God he'll be poorly then.'

Up to the age of seven I was tutored at home by Aunt May. After that I started going to the local church school, by which time Aunt May had a couple of young men paying calls on her. They were allowed to take her to the moving pictures or 'house dances'. One was Ridley, a foppish young man, and I disliked him immensely, and took pleasure in annoying him. As soon as his hat and cane were deposited on the hat rack in the hall, I would contrive to hide them. If he left the parlour for any reason, on his return there would be a 'flying horse' waiting in his chair for him. 'A flying horse' was an ordinary pin bent in such a manner that it sat with its point upward from the seat of the chair. Once the unwary victim sat down and made contact, he would be up again like a shot, and with much pain.

Then there was John John. I never quite knew why he was called John John because his name was neither John, nor Johnson. Whatever the answer to that little mystery, John John and I got on famously. John John never talked down to me as Ridley did, and he always had a special greeting for me. What is more, he invariably found time to tell me a story, or teach me a new card trick. He was good at letting cards disappear, and it was he who taught me how to cut my own 'top' from the root of a logwood tree and smooth it down with bits of broken glass without cutting myself. Yes, John John was tops in more ways than one. I used to pray every night that Aunt May would marry him, and that he would come to live with us. But, alas, that was never to be.

Soon Aunt May went to work in Kingston, and in a very short time after that went to Havana, Cuba, where her firm had a branch of their business. Whilst in Cuba, she sent me many lovely presents. The best loved of all was a two-piece outfit of sailor-blue trimmed with white. The trousers buttoned on to the blouse with large white buttons, and the pockets of the blouse had an anchor monogram made of braid. The first time I wore this grand outfit to Sunday School the other boys were green with envy, and that made me feel very important and superior.

The next time I saw Aunt May, some three or four years later, she had a husband (not my adored John John) but someone I

had never seen before. She also had a small baby, my cousin
Stanford, and I was not at all pleased. I could not bring myself to
like my Uncle Lattimer, although I adored Stanford. This
question of grown ups having babies had always puzzled me. It
seemed that whenever someone went away, on their return
there would be a baby, and I was told it had come from the
North Pole by sea. Now here was Aunt May with a baby. True
they had come by ship, but from Cuba, not the North Pole. It
was all very confusing to me.

Those early years at school were a very happy period for me. I
think I can honestly say I was bright without being brilliant,
never below the first four in my class. I loved games, was a fair
leg break bowler, and made the school's eleven for two out of
three seasons before going to college. I also represented my
school in athletics and swimming when I went to live with
Mamma in Port Maria. During this period Moma gave up the
shop (I never knew why) and also went to Cuba where she
worked demonstrating new kitchen equipment. But my first
sporting love was football; in this I really excelled. I was several
years later, to occupy the position of 'left half' in the Linstead
Football Club and the Jamaica Railway's second eleven, and
had the distinction of playing against the military at Up Park
Camp and the visiting Corinthian Casuals.

In between lessons and sports, there were the holidays which
were mainly spent in the country with relations. There was
Uncle Alex (that's my mother's uncle) who owned some 200
acres of farmland in the parish of St Mary. A typical day in the
country would begin with a visit to the milking sheds at six in the
morning, where we would have a mug of fresh milk still warm
from the udders. Breakfast at 7.30 consisting of roasted
breadfruit, or green plantain with butter, roast pork and a large
mug of coffee sweetened with condensed milk. About 9 o'clock
there would be a bare-backed ride to the river on horses or mules
using banana bark as reins. Once at the river we would undress,
place our clothes behind a big boulder and go for a swim in the
nude. The branches of trees overhanging the river were used as
improvised spring boards to dive into the 'blue hole', so called
because it reflected the blue of the sky overhead, and was very
deep. The much loved, but dangerous, game of 'Cork' would be
played. 'Cork' as its name implied, was a game played with a

10

cork. The basic idea was quite simple.

The assembled company would form a semi-circle, then one preselected member would plunge one or both hands containing the cork below the surface agitating the water vigorously, then let the cork fall. Whoever caught it as it returned to the surface would describe a somersault, coming down as quickly and heavily as he could with both feet extended in the opposite direction to that from which he entered the water. The remainder of the players would scatter as quickly as possible to avoid being hit by his descending feet. As the game was usually played beyond standing depth, this was not as easy as it sounds. I have known boys to be knocked unconscious, or have an ear or nose split, when they have been unlucky enough to make contact with a sharp toenail.

By the time swimming was over it would be lunch time, but in the country one very rarely has a cooked meal at midday. So we would lunch on mangoes, pineapple, sour-sop, star apple, or any other kind of fruit that was available in the area, and there were usually a dozen different varieties to choose from. The pangs of hunger satisfied, we would gather our guns or catapults (according to age) and shooting bags and leave for the forest to shoot birds. With the breeze rustling the trees overhead, the song of nightingales, the coo of pea-doves and white-wings in our ears, we would tread gently on the carpet of dried leaves underfoot, mindful not to disturb the objects of our quest.

With the sun dipping over the horizon, we would wend our weary way home in the fast descending tropical darkness. Our bags may not have been impressive, but we felt we had lived, and knew how good it was to be alive.

On other occasions when rain made the usual routine impossible, my cousins, their friends and myself would gather in one of the many barns used for storing corn or coffee beans. I would then entertain them with card tricks learnt from John John, or demonstrate to them the manly art of boxing, which for some unaccountable reason was never seriously indulged by country-bred youths in Jamaica.

As the saying goes, all good things must come to an end, or as Moma would say, 'too much of a good thing one for nothing'. The decision, which had been pending for some time, was taken to send me to college. I would be going to St Mary's College,

11

Port Maria, and Moma of course would be paying the fees. Perhaps I should mention here that St Mary's College was a public school run by the Catholic church, but unlike here in England, in Jamaica it was called a 'private school'.

There was one holiday I had in Kingston just before leaving college which also stands out in my memory. Three friends and myself, Ken, Vivian and Joe, set out in a hired flat bottomed boat from 'Breezy Castle' wharf for a night's fishing. We rowed to Port Royal about seven miles across the bay, and spent the night fishing from the old look-out tower at Fort George. The same fort from which Sir Henry Morgan and his cut-throat buccaneers used to sail to plunder 'merchantmen' along the Spanish Main. Among our night's catch was a four foot barracuda, one of the most vicious predators of the Caribbean coast.

Early next morning we set out for the tiny island of 'Lyme Quay'. It was a beautiful tropical morning with the sun overhead and the sea as calm and smooth as a mill pond. At the island we fished for several hours catching a number of mullets, flounders, and long-jaws. We then swam to a large rock about 200 yards away to dive for 'Kunks'. Whilst thus occupied we noticed a continuous stream of fishermen's boats heading for Port Royal and Kingston It occurred to us that they were returning rather early, but we attached no particular significance to the fact. This we soon discovered was because of our ignorance of the weather signs. About 11 o'clock it began to rain a steady downpour, and the clouds got suddenly very dark, and a heavy sea began to run.

Then, and only then, did we realise the danger we were in, and decided to high tail it back to the safety of Port Royal. This was to prove far more difficult than we had imagined it would be. In fact we were destined never to reach Port Royal. The heavy current and the strong wind which had got up in the mean time, kept carrying us away from Port Royal, and towards Port Henderson, about 10 miles to the west. The sea, which only a short while before was running in heavy swells, had now become a succession of mountainous waves which threatened to engulf us at any minute as our little craft was shipping water at an alarming rate. To add to our discomfiture, we had only one small calabash with which to bale the water out.

Then it happened; a mighty wave, the biggest one so far, hit us full broadside and our craft turned turtle sending us plunging below the surface. By the time we came up from the depths again, the swiftly moving current had taken the boat well out of our reach and going even further away all the time, not that it would have made very much difference as I doubt very much if we would have been able to right it in that cauldron of a sea. The nearest point of refuge from our present position was the 'East Light Buoy' marking one position of the channel entrance to Kingston harbour, and that was at least three quarters of a mile away. We would have to make it to that buoy somehow; it was our only chance of survival. Fortunately we were all very good swimmers and superbly fit from playing various games. As for myself the distance was not beyond my capability, as it was a regular pastime of mine to swim from the shore to the island about the same distance at my home town of Port Maria, the only difference was, those swims were always undertaken in perfect weather conditions.

I learnt in the next few hours how it is possible for the human body to raise itself to unsuspected heights of achievement when the only alternative is death. Made it we did somehow, but on more than one occasion Ken, who was the smallest, was on the point of giving in. However, whenever this happened, Vivian and Joe, who were bigger and older than Ken and myself, supported the lad between them. We eventually reached the buoy about two in the afternoon, as near as I could guess, and wrapped our arms around the lower sections of the wooden structure mounted on top of a deeply imbedded concrete base, and bearing the 'flashing beacon'.

We did not have the energy to try and climb to the top at once, but after two of us were torn from our precarious hold and had to battle our way back, it became obvious that, if we were to survive, we had to get to the top of the buoy. Vivian suggested that Ken, who was the lightest, should climb on his shoulders, whilst he, Vivian, trod water and I and Joe kept him as stable as possible. Ken could then reach far enough up to link his arms around one of the wooden legs supporting the light. We managed this, and after a brief rest I used Ken's dangling legs to pull myself into the same position. In this manner, one by one, we all got to the top of the buoy.

We remained there for what seemed an eternity, hungry, but most of all very thirsty as we had all swallowed quite a lot of sea water. About 5 o'clock that evening the Coaling Station Launch 'Enid' taking workmen back to Kingston from Port Royal spotted us. If its occupants had failed to spot us we would have had to spend a very uncomfortable night wet, hungry and thirsty on that buoy, because we would never have been able to call out loud enough to be heard above the din of the howling wind and waves beating against out refuge. Besides, in another half an hour no one would have been able to see us in the rapidly descending tropical night, which is always pitch dark.

We were taken aboard the launch in a state of near exhaustion, and it was then that we were told that the 'harbour police launch' had been out looking for us after being alerted by the fishermen who had passed us at Lyme Quay and realised that there was no way we could have made it back on our own. The police had also alerted all craft in the area to keep a sharp look-out for us. That experience, and a number of less spectacular occurrences since coming to England, have convinced me that I am one of life's survivors. It has left me with a firm conviction that no battle is ever lost, however hopeless it may seem, until the very last shot is fired. In short, my abiding philosophy is: 'Never give up whatever the odds'.

College, whilst pleasant enough, was never the same as my days at the local church school in St Ann's Bay, and later the government school. I played the usual games and was able to maintain a place in both the cricket and football teams. Lessons were a drudge to be endured because one's parents expected a 'pass' in the Local Cambridge Examinations for the next three years. Mathematics was the bane of my life. I was convinced that the chap who invented them should have been certified and put away for inflicting such abominations on the already ill-used student fraternity. But even I in the end came to appreciate the usefulness of this branch of learning.

At this time Mamma was employed as the housekeeper at Brimmer Hall, which was the country seat of the then Member of the island's Legislative Council representing the parish of St Mary. He was of course an ex-patriate Englishman. This august gentleman, who was a bachelor, spent most of his time in Kingston while the House was sitting, coming home only at the weekends. Mamma's chief function was to run the house and staff in his absence. To see that the place was in good order at all times, particularly during the shooting season when there would be several parties to cater for.

About 18 months after I became a student at St Mary's one of my college friends, the son of a local businessman, invited me to his birthday party at his home at Little Bay, a couple of miles from Port Maria. At the end of the evening his mother asked the parents of another school friend who had to pass Brimmer Hall on their way home to give me a lift home. On the way, these bigoted white pillars of local society questioned me as to my parentage and the fact that I was headed for Brimmer Hall. Simple me naturally told them that my mother was the housekeeper at Brimmer Hall. You can imagine our surprise when about a fortnight later my mother received a letter from the principal of my school asking her to call at the school alone on the following Monday morning, and that I was not to attend school again before the visit took place. Mamma's first reaction was to enquire what mischief I had been up to? But I was just as mystified as she was as to the reason for the summons.

To cut a long story short, Mamma was told that a number of parents had approached the principal and given an ultimatum that, 'unless I was removed from the school immediately, they and their friends would boycott the school by withdrawing all their children as they were not prepared to have their children mixing on equal terms with the son of a domestic servant employed by one of their social group'. The principal very much regretted the need to do so, but had no choice but to ask Mamma to remove me although I was showing great promise. My fees for that term would of course be refunded. 'How very generous!' Not only was the school dependent on their goodwill, but the school governors were without exception friends of the boycott group, and had intimated that they would support the boycott.

I was so disgusted and humiliated that I vowed I would never again attend a school in Jamaica. What is more, I would from then on make every conscious effort to lay as many of their precious daughters as it was possible to do. In that respect at least I can state that I had quite some revenge, but to this day the bitterness of that humiliation still rankles. My college days

15

having been brought to such a sudden and ignominious end through no fault of my own, I went to Linstead, where my Grandma had recently bought a new home and settled after disposing of the property in St Ann's Bay.

In Linstead I obtained a post as a salesman in a local drapery store for a short while, but soon gave that up to work for a solicitor as his clerk. While living and working in Linstead I joined the football club, and, as mentioned before, had a number of representative games with them. I also became First Vice President of the Linstead Literary and Debating Society. I have always had a natural flair for words and the marshalling of facts, and, although I say so myself, was a pretty formidable debater at that level. For the whole period of my membership of the debating society I never once lost a moot in which I was the mover.

My job with the solicitor I found very absorbing and rewarding, and I began to toy with the idea of taking up law as a career. My employer gave me every encouragement, and I had hopes of one day going to England to pursue my ambition. It had to be England because I had already vowed never to enter another educational establishment in Jamaica, and I did not think I could fit into the American Jim Crow pattern of the day. With this in mind I started a correspondence course with the Bennett College of London to try and qualify for my matriculation as a stepping stone to my eventual study of law. Then right out of the blue my mentor accepted a post with the Supreme Court of Jamaica and gave up his private practice. Once again my educational ambitions were thwarted.

As Linstead no longer offered any opportunities in which I was seriously interested I decided to move on, and followed my former employer to the big city. Although Moma was far from happy about my decision to abandon the country for the bright lights of Kingston, she nevertheless arranged accommodation for me with an old friend, whose children were about or near my own age. My new home was with a Mrs Williams, a widow, and her three children, a girl a bit older than myself and two boys one of whom, Ken, was the same age as myself, and who became a firm friend until his death some years after the war.

CHAPTER 2. *Life in the Big City.*

The big question for me now was, where do I go from here? Ken was the person who would answer that question for me, but neither of us knew it then. He was at that time employed as a 'floor walker', in English terms, a floor supervisor at a branch of one of the two leading haberdashers in the city. Common to all the leading business houses, they had their own sports club and grounds, and were involved in the cricket and football business house league competitions. Although Ken was not a participating sportsman, he would take me along to the club house and grounds from time to time for a game of cards or table tennis, or to watch a practice game of football or cricket. On one such occasion one of the centre halves involved in a practice game sustained an injury just before half time and had to leave the field. Since there was no replacement his side finished the first half with only ten men.

During the interval I spotted an old cricketing friend at the bar and went over for a chat and a drink. This friend, thinking I was an employee of the firm, shouted across the floor of the bar to one of the players, or maybe it was to one of the club officials, that there was a good left half kicking his heels at the bar. 'Why not let him sub for the second half?' I protested that I had no strip to change into knowing full well that if his suggestion was taken up, they would soon provide me with the necessary gear.

I was so anxious to have a game, I deliberately refrained from mentioning the fact that I was only a visitor and did not work for the firm. Just like that, I found myself taking part in the game for the second half after a slight re-shuffle of positions. I must have impressed someone of influence with my standard of play because after I had showered and changed I was approached by the club's secretary who wanted to know which department or branch of the firm I worked for as he would like to give me a trial. When I told him that I was only a visitor, and in fact was unemployed at the time, I was immediately asked to visit the firm's head office on the following Monday morning to see the personnel officer with a view to joining the company, in order to qualify as a member of the sports club, and therefore be eligible to play in the competition if selected.

The following Monday morning I duly presented myself as requested, and was immediately conducted to the personnel office. The interview that followed, if it could be honoured by that term, lasted about 25 minutes, and for 20 of those minutes the conversation centered almost exclusively around football. The personnel officer in his day was a goalkeeper of no small ability, a Calabar Old Boy who played for several years in the Manning Shield competition. Towards the end of the interview, almost as an afterthought, I was offered a job in the invoice department and told I could start work that very same day. Thus started what was to be a very happy association for me. In a very short time I was again playing the game I loved most, and in my favourite position of 'left half'. As my game progressed and the team crept up the league table, so my position with the firm improved, until other firms started vying for my services. Inevitably I accepted the offer of a better salary from a firm of manufacturers' representatives in the patent medicine and perfumery business.

With my enhanced earnings I decided I could afford to buy myself a motor cycle. The bike would serve a double purpose, apart from the obvious one of getting me to and from work. At the week-ends I was able to travel to various beauty spots or to dances out of town. I was also able to pay more frequent visits to Moma in Linstead and Mamma in Port Maria. I had also acquired a bit of a reputation as a 'ladies man', and was in great demand at week-end house parties.

By the middle of 1941 I was travelling the island as sales representative for my firm, and was to continue doing so until joining the Royal Air Force in 1943. From the moment I saw the film 'In Which We Serve', I had made up my mind that no self-respecting able-bodied young man could honourably remain at home when the fate of the world was literally at stake in Europe. Besides I had a sneaking admiration for the fighting spirit and courage of the British nation, although I had very little time for the average British colonial official and their creole offspring in the island.

The life of a travelling salesman, though tedious at times,

having to live out of a suitcase, putting up with indifferent meals and services in out-of-the-way hotels and boarding houses, nevertheless had its compensations, and I was not one to miss out on my share.

My itinerary was to cover the west and north of the island in about ten days, returning to Kingston for a week and sometimes even for a week-end just to play in a game, before setting out again for the south and east coast circuit. On the former run, Montego Bay with its excellent hotels and bathing beaches formed the main base of my operations. From there I would radiate to points east, west, north and south, returning each evening to enjoy the delights of, even in those far off days, one of the most famous holiday resorts in the world.

Montego Bay, as all travellers to the Caribbean will know, has some of the most superb white sand beaches to be found anywhere. On many a tropical moon-lit night, I could be found at Doctor's Cave or one of the other equally fabulous beaches of the area.

On other occasions it might be a drive, with the hood of the car down to get the full benefit of the sea breezes, to the 'Great House' at Rose Hall. Then again the scene would probably change, and it would be dancing to the hot tempo of a Jamaican calypso band, or the seductive strains of a waltz in one of the many night spots of the resort. On the return journey to Kingston the car would invariably be well stocked with fruits, vegetables and flowers showered on me by one or the other of my amorous conquests and her family.

One of my periodical out of town leisure trips was to visit a girl friend in Labyrinth, in the parish of St Mary. The route to Labyrinth was by way of the hair raising 'Devil's Race Course', so called because of its dangerous geography. This notorious highway starts a few miles north of the town of Linstead, and winds its narrow treacherous way upwards for several miles. On one side the road is bounded by a very high bank of scrub and vegetation, and on the other, a sheer drop of two hundred or more feet, either into a dry gully of peasant plantations, or timber houses precariously perched on the side of the cliff, low down. This road is so narrow in parts that it is impossible for two vehicles to pass abreast. Very often it is necessary for one or other of two vehicles to reverse quite a distance until a cut recess on the banked side of the road is reached to facilitate the act of passing. Jamaican drivers are renowned for their dare-devil driving, and almost total disregard of speed limits and road discipline.

To encounter one of this breed along the Devil's Race Course, as I did from time to time, was enough to add several years to my age and grey hairs to the head, always assuming that one is fortunate enough to survive the encounter unscathed. Although I was never actually involved in a serious accident on this ill-starred road, I had however many a narrow escape. One in particular when I was obliged to hurriedly vacate the seat of my motorcycle whilst it went hurtling over the edge of the precipice.

Besides having a girl friend in Labyrinth, I also had a number of distant relations living in the area. In fact about 80 to 85 percent of the village population were descended from my mother's side of the family. My great, great, great grandfather once owned the entire district, so I am told, and fathered some sixteen children by different mothers ranging from the local school marm down to his housekeeper and pantry maid. Old Busha, as he was called, was typical of the unmarried English gentry of the period, who had no hesitation in going to bed with the native women, but would never marry one. Nevertheless, when he died all his property was divided among his illegitimate children in his will.

Whenever I visited the area one of my relations would provide accommodation, and yet another would put a horse or mule at my disposal. Being a small farming community with very narrow streets, the use of motorised transport was always a danger to the many farm animals crossing the roads from one field to another, hence the need for a horse or mule as the case may be.

On one such occasion my ego was rudely deflated by one of my mounts. It was a sunny Sunday afternoon and I was riding to pay a call on the village post mistress, whom I hoped to number among my conquests. While some distance from my destination I could see the object of my visit seated with a number of her friends on the verandah of her house overlooking the road on which I was approaching. In order to impress them I immediately broke into a brisk gallop intending to pull up with a grand flourish just outside the house. Instead of reducing the speed of approach before reaching the house, I continued at full gallop and attempted to pull up suddenly in front of my admiring audience. In answer to my hard pull on the bridle my mount pulled up all right, but so sharp was the horse's response to my bidding, I was catapulted out of the saddle and landed in a most undignified heap in the middle of the road.

What was even worse, I landed so hard on my backside I was unable to pick myself up unaided. Fortunately I sustained no serious injury, but it was some time before my wounded pride was healed. Accidents apart, those visits to the countryside were a source of great joy to me, providing, as they did, feminine companionship and most-favoured-guest treatment from my rustic relations. Then there were the 'Diggings' when several families would combine to assist one family to gather the yam or sweet potato harvest. The best part of these gatherings from my point of view was the fare, which would consist of curried goat and plain boiled rice, or roasted chicken, and sometimes even a suckling pig with roasted yams and sweet potatoes, cooked over an open range and washed down with lashings of rum and coconut water.

In about September of 1942, in view of the decision which I had made to volunteer for war service, I felt I should have one last fling by visiting some of my favourite beauty spots and places of historical interest before taking the final plunge. Because, after all, it was quite possible I would never again have the opportunity to do so. With my current girl friend Sylvia I set out to visit Dunn's River Falls on the first leg of my journey of rediscovery.

The journey to Dunn's River was by way of Fern Gully, that natural arcade of ferns of every conceivable variety. Trees on either side of the narrow gorge road overlapped, shutting out the sun and daylight, so that even on the brightest day there is a twilight darkness about the place that gives it an eerie enchantment. The smell of ferns, wild flowers, mint, ram-goat-dash-along and cirocee vie constantly for supremacy.

From Fern Gully our journey took us on to the lovely fordings of Windsor, which cross and re-cross the road no less than eight times, hence the Spanish name of Ocho Rios (eight rivers) given to the market town of the area. Stopping from time to time, we gathered and ate mangoes of many different varieties that grew in profusion along our route. We arrived at Dunn's River, or

21

Rio Nuevo, to give it its Spanish name, in the early afternoon, and immediately set out to climb the falls.

It is not enough to merely visit Dunn's River, you must also climb the falls as my companion and I did, before you can truly claim to have visited Dunn's River. The river starts from a wooded glade high up in the hills, disappears under the road, only to emerge again lower down, flowing over ledges of rocks below where it forms beautiful pools of water ideal for bathing; but it does not stop there because it plunges down over yet more rocks, to finally end up on the white sandy beach below.

On any week-end or public holiday, many of the island's most beautiful girls of every shade of colour, can be seen mingling with the American and European tourists arrayed in the latest New York, London or Paris swim wear. A visit to Dunn's River for the male of the species is not only a pleasant form of relaxation, but also a feast of feminine optical delight not to be missed.

From Dunn's River we travelled on to St Ann's Bay where I took the opportunity to visit some old family friends and relations. The following day we paid a visit to Sevilla, which is only about a quarter of an hour's drive west of the town. Sevilla is the spot where the Spaniards first set foot on the island. In the year 1510 Don Juan de Esquival, a Spanish general serving under Christopher Colombus's son-in-law in Hispanola, landed a small party and settled a colony near the spot where Colombus himself was marooned some years earlier. The site of the new colony was named Sevilla Nueva (New Seville). The settlers erected a church and other buildings on the site, and it's believed started to build a governor's residence but apparently were never able to complete it. The ruins were excavated by the Institute of Jamaica and it is now a great tourist attraction, but that was some time after the present visit.

The area was swampy and very unhealthy, and most of the settlers soon caught the dreaded fever. Within five years the survivors were forced to move out. They travelled inland across the island and set up a new colony at St Jago-de-la-Vega (St James-in-the-Vale). This site was later to become the Spanish capital of the island, and is to this day known as Spanish Town.

Spanish Town, even today, is a mixture of ancient beauty and modern squalor. The squalor is to be found in its cheap timber houses and narrow dirty streets, and beauty in its magnificent cathedral, the oldest church on the island, the old King's House (built in 1762), and the Rodney Monument, erected around 1790. These buildings were all situated in the famous Square, which has been referred to as 'the most striking collection of 18th century buildings in the world',* and rightly so.

From Sevilla Nueva we left the coast road just as our Spanish forerunners had done, and travelled inland through Brown's Town and Cave Valley up to Christiana where we spent the night. The next day we set out across rough terrain for Accompong, the old Maroon settlement in the Cockpit Country, what historic memories the name evokes? Somewhere around the late 1690's or early 1700's a large number of slaves attacked their masters and fled into the mountains of Trelawny, known as the Cockpit Country (no doubt because of its rocky and precipitous nature). They were led by Accompong, who was later joined by two other runaway slaves named Cuffee and Cudjoe whom, it is believed, were tribal leaders before being tricked into slavery by British slave traders. Even at the time of our visit this area was still very inaccessible. A sturdy car, with luck, might have got as far as Look Behind. Beyond there the journey had to be made on foot or horse back.

The road, or rather path would be a more accurate description, wound its way along huge crags with precipices of considerable depth in parts. A small band of desperate and armed men, as the escaped slaves were, could, and did hold this territory against the might of the British army. The slaves regularly raided the low land plantations at night to steal food. Whenever they did this they would murder the occupants and burn the buildings, returning to their mountain hide-out before they could be caught.

The planters and the government became so alarmed at the activities of the Maroons, as the escaped slaves had come to be called, that in 1710, a law was passed whereby any slave who attacked his master or attempted to escape would have a hand or foot amputated for the first offence, both arms or both legs for the next offence, and so on, as an example to anyone else who

---

*Encyclopaedia Britannica.

might be tempted to do the same. In spite of this inhuman brutality, more and more slaves escaped to join their free brethren. It is a fact that no punishment or torture has yet been devised that will deter men who truly value their freedom.

Before long the number of free slaves in the mountains numbered over two thousand. In 1730, two regiments of troops were brought from Europe in an attempt to dislodge the Maroons; this however failed completely. The soldiers were no match for the Maroons due to their lack of knowledge of the terrain. The escaped slaves waged a constant guerilla warfare for three years, then martial law was declared and more troops brought in. The soldiers had some initial success when a small party of Maroons were ambushed and surprised. Those who survived rejoined the main body of guerilla slaves. Whenever the soldiers attacked after that the Maroons were always prepared, and it was the soldiers who were continually routed.

The authorities then tried to dislodge the Maroons by using 'Mosquito Indians', imported from Honduras to track them down, but the Indians had no better luck than did the soldiers. Utterly exhausted by their efforts to conquer the Maroons, the government, under the humane leadership of Sir Edward Trelawny (after whom the territory was later named), the then governor, made peace with them. In 1739 a treaty was signed with the Maroons on behalf of the British government, giving the Maroons and their successors that part of the island which they had defended so valiantly. They were to hold it free of tax. They were also given the right to make their own laws and try their own cases. In short, complete self-government within their limited confines.

If a Maroon committed a crime he could only be tried by his own chief, the British civil authority on the island would have no jurisdiction over him, except in cases of murder or treason which carried the death penalty, and had to be reviewed by the governor. When one remembers that we are talking about the achievements of a band of bare-footed escaped slaves in 1739, fully a hundred years before slavery was abolished, it will be appreciated how fantastic was their accomplishment.

Some fifty years after the treaty, two Maroons were flogged for stealing; this was done by the planters from whom the stealing was done, in breach of the terms of the treaty. The

Maroons protested that they should have been allowed to try and punish the culprits themselves. The acting-governor, the Earl of Balcarres, angrily dismissed their protests as presumptious. The Maroons were also at that time pressing for a review of the treaty, with a view to obtaining more and better arable lands for their growing population. The governor used this as an opportunity to abrogate the treaty altogether. Several thousand troops were sent in against the Maroons. That was not all, he went even further by copying the methods of the Spaniards in Cuba. Bloodhounds were imported into the island to help the soldiers hunt down the Maroons.

Black effigies were made of straw and the stomachs filled with food. The dogs were trained to attack the stomachs of the effigies to obtain the hidden food. Consequently when a Maroon was located, the hounds would immediately proceed to tear his stomach open. Even with this latest barbarity, the campaign lasted for many months before the Maroons were forced to sue for peace. Here we come to one of the most discreditable actions perpetrated by an English official in the West Indies. After a fresh treaty was signed with the Maroons guaranteeing that no reprisals would be taken against them once they had laid down their arms, the governor cynically ordered the arrest of the Maroon leaders. This, in spite of his own signed agreement, and had them deported to Nova Scotia. In Nova Scotia the Maroons were no less defiant than they had been in Jamaica.

They refused to do work of any kind, and the Jamaican government had to support them. After three years the governor refused to continue paying for their keep and they were shipped back to Sierra Leone in Africa. They at least were back in their native land. The Maroons still in Jamaica had lost their leaders, but they were allowed to remain in their mountain homes, where Sylvia and I were able to talk and joke with their descendants. Had we been white, or for any reason been suspected of being government agents, our reception would have been anything but friendly.

From the Maroon settlement we went on to Kingston passing through Spanish Town on the way. We did not tarry in Kingston but went on to Morant Bay, a town on the east coast of the island. There was not a lot to see in Morant Bay, but the Court House was the scene of one of the bloodiest and most controversial epics in the long history of oppression in Jamaica. In the year 1864, a Baptist missionary, the Reverend Dr Edward Underhill, paid a visit to Jamaica, and on his return to England wrote a letter to the Colonial Office protesting at the harsh treatment of the natives in Jamaica. The letter was passed to Governor Eyre asking for an explanation. Although the governor denied the allegations in the letter, he nevertheless had it published in the island's press. A mulatto named William Gordon, the son of a white planter and his negro mistress, and a lay preacher named Paul Bogle took up where Underhill's letter left off.

They held meetings all over the island encouraging the native population to protest at their treatment. These meetings were called 'Underhill Meetings' after the writer of the letter. Several representations were made to the authorities by these two men on behalf of the people, but the governor just ignored them. Bogle and his followers marched from Morant Bay to Spanish Town, the capital, a distance of nearly 40 miles to present a petition to the governor. When they got there the governor refused to see them. They were forced to march all the way back to Morant Bay without a hearing; by then they were a very angry and dangerous body of men. On their return Bogle began secretly to train his followers for an uprising without the knowledge of his partner Gordon, who lived in Kingston and was a member of that city's Council.

In either September or October of 1865, Bogle and a party of his supporters invaded the town of Morant Bay and rescued a man whom the police were trying to take into custody for causing a disturbance at the court house. The local authority asked for troops to be provided to take in Bogle and his men. In the meantime Bogle, who had no intention of quietly waiting around for the troops to come and get him, again marched into Morant Bay at the head of an army of his supporters armed with stolen guns and machettes. They marched to the front of the court house and, when asked to disperse, refused to do so. The handful of soldiers who were present opened fire on the protesters in a moment of apparent panic. Bogle and his men then rushed the court house, set it on fire, and murdered the court officials as they tried to flee the burning building.

After this they rampaged over the parish burning buildings

26

and plantations. Martial law was declared and more troops sent in. In retaliation for the few officials who were murdered at the court house, six hundred natives were either shot, bayoneted, hanged or flogged to death in the open streets, and a thousand natives homes burnt down. The ringleader Bogle and his partner Gordon, who was brought from Kingston although he had taken no part in the rebellion and knew nothing of its planning, were both given a farcical trial and were hung the same day in the court house where they were tried. A clear case of judicial lynching (certainly in the case of Gordon) if ever there was one. Eventually a Royal Commission was appointed to enquire into the cause of the rebellion and the methods used to put it down.

In their report they found that the cause of the rebellion was bad administration, and the methods used to put it down were unjustifiably severe; that the men, Bogle and Gordon, were not given a fair trial. Finally, the governor was recalled and relieved of his commission. So ended one of the bloodiest annals of the island's history. Walking those quiet peaceful streets and admiring the colourful peasant dress of the country women going to and from market, I found it hard to believe that such wanton slaughter and brutality actually took place on the very streets I was then treading. And by a British administration supposedly set up in the first place to protect the natives from the exploitation of the white planters.

On the way back to Kingston I was rather preoccupied with my thoughts for the first part of the journey, so much so that my companion had to ask what was worrying me? 'Not worried', I replied, 'just thinking'. What of? The apparent inability of governments to learn or profit from the lessons of the past. Take the incidents we have just been recalling, one would hardly expect any future British administration in the island to miss the lessons of that rebellion. Yet a mere 73 years later, in 1938 to be precise, another British governor again called out the troops and declared a state of emergency to put down a popular and just demand for more work and better working conditions.

The troubles of 1938 really began in 1937 when some of the workers at Gray's Inn sugar factory refused to continue gathering the crop because they considered their wages were too low. Those workers who refused to join the stoppage were given police protection to the end of the harvest. In January 1938 labourers employed at Serge Island sugar estate were being paid 10½d (old money) per ton to cut the sugar cane; they downed tools and demanded 2/- (10p new money) per ton. Their demand was at first refused, but after struggles with the police, in which some 30 or 40 people were injured and many workers arrested, an offer of 1/- (5p) per ton was accepted and work resumed.

In April of that year, the workers at Frome estate in Westmoreland, in addition to a demand for higher wages and better working conditions, asked to be paid on a Friday instead of Saturday evening, so that their families' foodstuff could be bought before the shops closed for the weekend. The management refused their very reasonable requests and ordered the workers, who had gathered in the grounds of the estate, to disperse. The men refused to do so until the management agreed their just demands. Police reinforcements were brought in to supplement the estate guards. Enraged by this action the workers attacked the estate officers and the police opened fire. As a result, scores of workers were injured.

As soon as news of this reached the capital Kingston, Alexander Bustamante, ironically himself also a mulatto as George William Gordon had been, went poste haste to Frome to try and negotiate with the estate management on behalf of the workers, but this was to no avail. The management were not prepared to concede anything. For the next few weeks trouble flared up in many parts of the island in general sympathy for the workers of Frome, who were by now being tried and sentenced for the earlier disturbance. Kingston became the focal point for this movement of sympathy with marches by the port workers and municipal workers.

In a very short while almost all the unemployed in the city were on the march, invading local government offices, the sewage pumping station, and the main power station. Vehicles were overturned (including a tram car), all bus and train services were halted. On the 23rd May, at a meeting being addressed by Bustamante, the police ordered the listeners to move on; they refused and the officer in charge ordered his men to fire into the crowd. Immediately Bustamante stepped in front of the police rifles, opened his shirt, and ordered them to shoot him rather than the defenceless people. The police held their fire, and Bustamante and his listeners were able to walk away unharmed on that occasion.

That action assured Bustamante the complete loyalty of the workers from that day onwards. On the 24th May Bustamante was refused permission to hold a meeting, he nevertheless went ahead and he and his lieutenant, a man named Grant, were arrested and charged with inciting a civil disturbance. Bail was refused. This high handed action of the authorities so enraged the workers, that quite spontaneously workers all over the island downed tools. As a result complete chaos ruled. The governor, Sir Edward Denham, declared a state of emergency. This sparked off several running battles between the police and the strikers, and again the garrison was called out to assist the police.

The state of emergency lasted for several months, and thousands of special constables were sworn in to augment the forces of law and order. This became necessary, because as in all such situations, there were the purely criminal elements who used the emergency as a cover for their criminal activities, thereby doing damage to the cause of the geniune strikers. In spite of this complication, the strikers won their point in the end.

A Royal Commission was again appointed to enquire into the cause of the disturbance, and to make recommendations. As a direct result of their inquiry, a Labour Dispute Arbitration Board was set up and a Labour Exchange established where, for the first time, the unemployed could register for work. Relief works running into several millions of pounds were put into hand. Unionism was fostered and protected by law. For the first time in the island's history, a man's right to withhold his labour became a legal and constitutional right.

Finally, a new constitution was granted the island. In fact the colony was asked by the British government to draft the type of constitution it would like, after having turned down the one offered by the Royal Commission chairman, Lord Moyne. The chief architect in the drafting of the new constitution was that great son of Jamaica, the late J. A. G. Smith, affectionately remembered as 'JAGS', a leading West Indian barrister of the day. We had come a long way since 1938. By the 1950's it would have been impossible for any British governor of the island to order the garrison out without the prior approval of the island's

29

cabinet, whose Chief Minister was none other than the same Alexander Bustamante who had been jailed for his part in organising the workers in the 1938 disturbances.

Subsequent to the above events Jamaica achieved its independence from Britain, and its first Prime Minister, you've guessed it, was Bustamante. And Michael Manley, who first became Prime Minister in 1972, is in fact a second cousin of Bustamante.

To all West Indians be they first or second generation now settled in England I would say, when confronted by bigots and neo-Nazis who would dare to question your right to be here, just calmly point out the fact that their ancestors ravaged your homeland and exploited your forefathers for centuries in order to help put the 'Great' into Great Britain. That, apart from the fact that thousands of West Indians fought in this country against Nazi tyranny. Ten thousand in the Royal Air Force alone, and thousands more in the Army, Merchant Navy and Munitions Works which gives us the undisputed right to live in peace and share equally in the fortunes or otherwise of this country. More so than many of our critics or their parents who had no choice but to fight for survival. We on the other hand were all volunteers in a common cause with (as we erroneously thought) our white cousins. I make no apologies for this digression from the main theme of my narrative when I read in my daily paper of 'burning crosses' being thrown into the homes of Black people in this country, and see wall grafitti saying, 'Blacks go home'. In God's name, if this is not, where then is our home?

CHAPTER 3. *En Route to the War & Training in Yorkshire.*

In order to implement my decision to enlist in the armed forces of the Crown, I duly presented myself at the recruitment centre in Kingston where I was given an application form, told to take it away, complete and return it as soon as possible. This I did the very same day. Instead of being given a date to report to the local garrison for training as I expected, imagine my surprise and disappointment when I was told that my application would be considered by the appropriate authorities, and I would in due course be informed of their decision. I was absolutely livid. Did they need fighting men or not? If the newspapers and recruiting posters were to be taken seriously, there was need for every able-bodied man that could be induced to come forward, yet here was I, intelligent, willing and able, being told, 'your application will be considered in due course'.

If that was the measure of urgency with which the war was being prosecuted, I could not help but feel its duration would outlive my generation. As if to confirm my most pessimistic view, some three weeks later I received a letter directing me to report to a very well known school building, on a Saturday morning three days later to sit an educational test. It was yet another ten days before I was informed that I had satisfied the educational requirements, and was invited to meet the selection committee for an interview to decide for which branch of the armed forces I was best suited. On that score I had no doubts whatsoever, it was the Royal Air Force for me.

The selection committee, which consisted of an army officer, an officer of the Royal Air Force, and an elderly civilian gentleman, was a further projection of my not very flattering opinion of everyone and everything connected with the present venture. The two officers I understood, but the presence of the civilian rather intrigued me. I concluded he was there no doubt to see fair play between the two contesting claimants for my services. I later learnt that he represented the business

31

organisations of the island who were sponsoring and paying for our journey to England.

Somewhere between the latter part of 1942 and early 1943, a number of business organisations owned mostly by ex-patriate Englishmen decided that, as their contribution to the war effort, they would sponsor and finance a limited number of volunteers for the army and air force to fight in Europe. At that time no attempt was being made from official sources to tap the Jamaican manpower potential. The response to their initiative was so enthusiastic and overwhelming that I suspect the British Government was shamed into taking over the operation by instituting official recruitment of West Indian males for these two branches of the armed forces. Eventually there were about 10,000 West Indians serving in the Royal Air Force, about 70% of whom were Jamaicans. I do not have the figures for the army, but at a rough guess I would say there were perhaps as many as in the air force.

Not surprisingly then, it was the civilian who put the first question in his most pompous manner. 'Now young man, why do you want to join the armed forces?' I felt like saying, 'to start a conscientious objectors club'. Instead, I replied, 'to serve my King and Country'.

'Admirable, admirable my boy.' The pompous old ass, I thought. Now it was the turn of the army, 'Which branch of the service would you like to join? The army or the air force?' I wondered what would happen if I said the Navy. At that time 'negroes' were not being accepted into the Royal Navy. I replied however, 'the air force, sir'. 'We could really do with you in the army, you know, make a damned good soldier of you.' I had no intention of being manoeuvred into the army, and countered, 'I have no doubt whatever, sir, that whichever branch of the service I enter, I would be properly trained, but if the air force will have me, that's where I would like to be'.

'Excellent, that's the gen, give it to him straight. After that, Colonel, I think any further attempts to sell him to the army would be poaching.' 'Yes, I think this one is yours Squadron Leader.' 'Now Mr Noble (for the first time I was being addressed by name), you may return home and make your plans, as we shall be sending you to the Palisadoes base in about ten days time.' At this all three rose, indicating that the interview was at an end. Each in turn shook me by the hand, and wished me good luck. I was delighted, and perhaps for the first time in my life I was completely tongue-tied. 'Thank you sirs, er, I mean gentlemen.'

The very next day I departed for Port Maria to spend a few days with Mamma, before going on to Linstead to see my dear old Moma. I knew she would take my joining the forces very hard, and I wanted to spend the major part of my remaining time with her.

Mamma took the news in her stride, her main concern was that I should make sure I was always adequately covered up against the treacherous English weather. To hear her speak one would think there was perpetual winter in England.

Moma on the other hand was obviously broken hearted over my impending departure, but resolved not to blight my last visit with her by shedding tears (although I am sure she did so in private). Instead she spent the time knitting me a woollen pullover. In fact she was a member of the local War Effort Committee who sold raffle tickets, held jumble sales etc., to raise funds towards the upkeep of the Spitfire squadron which Jamaica had contributed to the war effort.

When my ten days at Linstead had expired and the time came to say goodbye, I found it far more difficult than I had imagined it would be. Moma was convinced that even if I survived the war, she would have passed away before I returned. So, for her at any rate, this meant a last and final farewell. This realisation upset me much more than I cared to admit. I had no fears for myself. With the supreme confidence of youth, I was sure I would return at the end of the war, decorated and be-medalled. It was the thought that I might really never see my beloved Moma again, which brought a lump to my throat, and tears to my eyes. If she had any fears for my life she certainly did not voice them. Typical of her deep understanding, she evinced more conern for my material comfort. 'Don't forget to wear lots of warm clothes, go to bed early, and stay away from loose women. Have regular meals, and write often.' 'Yes Moma, I will take care of myself, and I will write at least once per week.' How glibly those promises were given, and in all sincerity. But before long I was to discover that in total war, even such mundane acts as writing letters can be no longer a matter of one's own decision.

33

Once embarked on the troopship for England, although I wrote dutifully every week, it was to be more than three months before any of my letters were delivered. From the moment of embarkation, nay two days before that, there was a complete security blackout, until our safe arrival in England some three months later.

My instructions from the recruitment office were to report to Pallisadoes air base. On arrival I was directed to a small building where there were about a dozen young men like myself, in civilian clothes, and carrying large suit cases. We were apparently the last of that day's batch of recruits to arrive. After about a quarter of an hour, in which time I had introduced myself to the others, a corporal arrived and marched us, suit cases and all, to the kitting-out building. Each name was called in alphabetical order, given a number (by which we would be known for the remainder of our service life), and as we passed along a long counter, behind which a number of airmen were standing, each recruit was issued with a different item of kit or clothing by each airman.

Kitting-out having been completed, we were directed to various billets, to a pre-arranged plan, shown the dining hall, and informed that dinner would be served between 12.30 and 2 p.m., after which, we were to return to our respective billets and await further instructions. The remainder of that first day was spent handing in our civilian clothes which would be returned to our homes, and familiarising ourselves with the general lay-out of the base.

On the following day our initial training began in earnest, and continued uninterrupted for the next three weeks. Fortunately for me, playing football had kept me very fit. Nevertheless, for the first week at the end of each day, it was as much as I could do to write up my diary before retiring. For some of my comrades it was much, much worse. One or two were so completely done-in at the end of the day that they quite regularly went to bed without waiting for the evening meal.

Soon we sensed rather than knew, that the date of our departure could not be far off. Then one morning towards the end of the third week, instead of the usual drill routine, we were told on first parade, that we would be going on a week's leave starting that very afternoon. Leave pay and ration allowances

34

were collected, walking-out dress pressed where necessary, and all were ready to depart just after dinner. On the military transport into Kingston, the usual flights of fancy as to how this first leave would be spent, was given full rein.

My last farewell to the family was such a disturbing one that I decided quite deliberately not to visit them again before sailing. I refrained from mentioning the fact that I was on leave. So as not to arouse the family's suspicions, I wrote two letters and left them at the guard room, with instructions for their posting at three day intervals.

During this week in Kingston I spent a large part of my time at the public library, reading everything I possibly could about England and the English people. I wanted to learn all I could in the short time at my disposal, about the people with whom I would be living and fighting in the near future.

Two days after returning from leave, we were ordered to hand in our tropical kit and draw a supply of overseas kit from stores. We were forbidden to communicate with our families, or anyone outside the base. All passes were stopped, even for the permanent staff of the base. On the night of the fourth day we were marched in full battle order to Port Royal docks, where we boarded a troopship. We knew that our ultimate destination was England, beyond that, no other information was given to us.

Our first port of call was the American naval station at Guantanamo Bay in Cuba. No one was allowed ashore, and no one, certainly no one among the recruits, knew why we had called there. It could not have been for re-fuelling as we had only been at sea for a very few hours, and no more troops were taken on board. Local traders in a variety of small crafts laden with trinkets, straw hats, and a large assortment of fruits came along side plying their wares. Strict orders were given, however, that only fruit should be bought from them. The officers were obviously concerned that we should not encumber ourselves with a lot of useless acquisitions before entering the war zone.

For the next three days the voyage settled down to a calm and placid routine of exercise, meals and sleep, in that order. The sea was as smooth and unruffled as a mill pond. Then quite suddenly in the afternoon of the fourth day, the entire scene changed. An ominous silence descended on us, followed by a distant whistling which quite rapidly developed into a hideous roar, reminiscent of an express train rushing through a tunnel, to be followed by a crashing blast of thunder, and a colossal tropical downpour. The sea whipped by the wind, came at us in huge mountainous waves, which left the great troopship wallowing in their wake like a mere bit of flotsam.

The sound of breaking glass, slithering furniture, and the shouts of officers giving orders to the crew, adding to the general noise of the storm, created an unholy din. For most of us recruits this was a very frightening experience. Many could be seen hanging over the rails, their stomachs in revolt. As the evening progressed the wind gradually subsided, the sea became calmer, and the clouds gave way to a gentler, but steady fall of rain. By midnight the storm had blown itself out, and shipboard life returned to something like its normal routine as quickly as it had erupted.

We were disembarked at Newport News, given the luxury of a bath and a meal, before departing for a military camp near Denbigh, Virginia. On arrival at the camp, we joined, or were joined by a number of English airmen, who had been undergoing training in Canada, and like ourselves were in-transit to England. We spent a month at this camp (Camp Patrick Henry) and, considering that we were negroes almost to a man, in the heart of the American 'Jim Crow Country', our stay was a very pleasant one in every way.

As guests of the American government, and British subjects at that, we were more or less given the run of the camp. We shared all the social amenities that were available to the white Americans, and were even given a small spending allowance in dollars by Uncle Sam's government. The food, which is always a major consideration with servicemen the world over, was excellent, and there was plenty of it. There was, however, one aspect of our treatment which struck me as rather odd: the desperate attempts by everyone in authority (American that is) to try to convince us level headed West Indians that, simply because we were wearing the uniform of the Royal Air Force, we were somehow superior to the American negro, who was wearing the uniform of his own country; therefore that entitled us to more favoured treatment. How naive can one get?

Let it be clearly understood that no stone was left unturned by our American hosts to make our stay among them a comfortable

36

and enjoyable one. Visits to places of interest, including the factory of a world renowned brand of cigarettes, were laid on. In spite of all that, I left America with the distinct feeling that, as a negro, I had no great desire to return to it.

When we departed from Camp Patrick Henry, the train journey to Jersey City, though it gave only brief glimpses of the country, nevertheless afforded us an opportunity to see something of the general topography of that part of America. Some of it was very beautiful indeed, but what impressed me most was the sense of vastness which it conveyed. At Jersey City the train went straight on to the river boat for the trip across the Hudson River to New York. This was a completely new and thrilling experience for me and my friends. Accustomed as we were to the comparatively small rivers and boats of our tiny island home, we could never, until then, have envisaged a whole troop-train being transported by boat. This was to be the first of many such contrasts, which brought home to us, the minuteness and almost insignificance of Jamaica, in the context of the world as a whole.

New York when it was reached, as far as I am concerned, remains but a mere impression of docks and boats' sirens. As for the famous Statue of Liberty, we never saw it, because our ship sailed that same night whilst we were asleep after our long and exhausting journey half way across America. When we awoke next morning and went on deck, we beheld a convoy of some forty troopships and merchantmen, a destroyer and two frigates, our escorts, on the distant horizon.

The voyage to Liverpool was long, much too long, tedious and uncomfortable. The best that can be said for it is that we arrived safely. Two things however stand out in my memory from this voyage. An abiding abhorrence of sausage which has lasted to this day, having been forced to eat the ghastly things twice a day for ten consecutive days when we ran out of other provisions, due to our unexpected length of time at sea dodging German U-boats. The other was intense cold. Cold as I had never before experienced it or imagined it could be. Thankfully all things must sooner or later come to an end. So did this voyage. One morning in June the convoy nudged its way up the Mersey estuary to give us our first sight of England.

Liverpool, when it came into view, did not give a flattering

37

first impression. This was not surprising, after the hammering it had taken in the war so far. On disembarkation we were met by members of the Women's Volunteer Service (WVS), who served us with unsweetened tea and buns. Briefly refreshed, we were then shepherded aboard a troop-train bound for a training camp RAF Filey on the Yorkshire moors. On the journey we passed through the ancient and beautiful cathedral city of York, then on to Scarborough, one of the most popular north country holiday resorts. If the truth be told, by now we were in no fit state to observe or appreciate any of this beauty.

One of the first pleasant surprises England provided for me personally was the luxuriant vegetation of the countryside. The very last thing I expected to see in England was fields and gardens to rival in beauty the tropical growths of my native land. The trim vegetable and flower gardens, which adorned the backs of the houses facing the railway lines, were a welcome optical relief after weeks of monotonous sea and sky.

The camp which was reached in the late afternoon was much better than we had dared to hope. It was situated on a cliff overlooking the sea to the east. On the south-eastern side was a fairly large golf course. To the west, a cluster of neat semi-detached houses. To someone unaccustomed as I was to the English type of dwelling house, they looked like so many boxes, albeit, beautiful boxes, in a bee hive, each one being identical to its neighbour. I could imagine myself, after an indulgent night out on the town, being unable to identify my particular box. The thought of trying to gain entrance to my neighbour's house, expecially if the master happened to be away, brought an amused chuckle at the thought of what the wagging tongues, and prying eyes would make of it.

This was a basic training camp for Royal Air Force and Royal Air Force Regiment recruits. The site in peace time was a Butlin's holiday camp, but had no doubt been taken over by the War Office or Air Ministry after the outbreak of hostilities. My fellow recruits and I were by normal military standards, very comfortably billeted four to a billet in this erstwhile holiday camp. Ernest being the tallest and most well built of the four, was the natural choice as senior recruit in charge of our chalet. Not much chance of anyone bucking his authority. Ernest certainly commanded physical authority, but it was I who

38

immediately established myself as spokesman and trouble-shooter of the group. My very first self-imposed task was to get hold of a copy of King's Regulations and Air Council Instructions (KRI'S) from the camp library, in service parlance, the 'airman's bible'. The object of the exercise was to make myself thoroughly conversant with our rights, duties and obligations under current regulations. In a relatively short time I had become a sort of 'legal adviser' and 'father confessor' to my chalet mates. If a way had to be found around an irksome regulation, I found it. If an infringement of basic liberty took place, I would immediately spot it and take measures to have it redressed.

Among the other recruits I became the 'squadron leader' for the remainder of our training. The actual term used to describe me at the time was Squadron Leader Walrus. I was nicknamed Squadron Leader Walrus because within days of my arrival at RAF Filey I was forced to have three of my upper front teeth extracted. This left a yawning gap in the middle of my mouth, which in turn emphasised the prominence of the remaining teeth on either side, hence the resemblance to a walrus. It was inevitable that this role would bring me into conflict with the flight sergeant instructor. Whilst there was no real enmity in this encounter, the flight sergeant was an 'old sweat' who took pride in describing himself as a 'Liverpool dock rat', and was determined to cut this 'rookie upstart' down to size.

With the remainder of the flight, the very eminence of Flt. Sgt. Harper's rank was enough to put the fear of god into them. I, on the other hand, was determined to combat force of rank with intelligent strategy. Echos of my days as a solicitor's clerk. In this respect, every duty, every instruction, was meticulously carried out without question. In short, I strove to meet every standard set by my instructors, and was so successful in my dedicated application, that grudgingly the Flight Sergeant would from time to time use me to demonstrate to the 'awkward squad', how a particular manoeuvre in sentry-go or rifle drill etc. should be properly executed.

Towards the end of the second week of training, I decided I would go into Hunmanby Moor, the nearest village to our camp, on the Saturday night in spite of a quarantine which had been placed on us as soon as we arrived. This, however, meant

39

running the gauntlet of the flight sergeant. A way had to be found around this particular hazard. I had noticed that the flight sergeant was very friendly with a certain airwoman who worked in the airmen's mess. I therefore approached her with the story that the boys of my chalet and myself wanted to lay on a little surprise treat in one of the village pubs for the flight sergeant as soon as the quarantine was lifted, as a gesture of appreciation for his kind handling of us in our initial ignorance, but in order to maintain the element of surprise, we needed to know which pub he used, so that we could avoid him when making the arrangements.

However lame that excuse may seem now, it should not be forgotten that the white personnel on camp at the time had a very poor opinion (due to ignorance) of the black recruits. It was not at all surprising, therefore, that she believed every word, and was only too happy to cooperate in a harmless conspiracy by giving me the name and location of the public house which the flight sergeant frequented.

On the night of my choice I slipped under the wire, went to the village, and had myself a whale of a time in a pub well removed from the scene of the 'dock rat's' junketing. After breakfast the following morning, I again contacted the airwoman and informed her that, unfortunately, the little surprise we were planning would have to be called off, as we were reliably informed that senior NCOs were forbidden to drink with, or accept presents from, the recruits under their charge. This of course I was fully aware of all along. Not that it would have made the slightest difference to either the flight sergeant, or ourselves, if a genuine intent was present.

Shortly after the quarantine was lifted, I paid a visit to Scarborough on a day pass one Saturday. The afternoon was spent seeing the sights and enjoying a walk in Peasholme Park, where the flowers were already clad in their riotous summer colours, rivalled only by a variety of printed cotton dresses of the lovely Yorkshire lasses out for an afternoon and evening's enjoyment with the many servicemen who frequented the town. Scarborough was, up until then, the only large English town I had ever visited. On market day, even in war-time, it was a bustling busy place. Apart from servicemen, there were very few young men to be seen anywhere, but there were lots of girls, old men and middle-aged women, and a surprisingly large number of children. I elicited the information that the large number of children was due to the fact that this was one of the areas to which children from London and other vulnerable industrial and shipping areas were evacuated during the blitz.

On my walk almost everyone gave me a greeting, and some, more bold than others, even stopped for a chat. They wanted to know what part of the world I was from, and marvelled at the fact that I spoke English perfectly, and without any trace of a foreign accent. The high spot of my afternoon's walk for me was a darling old couple, who humbly begged to be allowed to shake my hand for luck. Until then I thought that sort of superstition was confined to uneducated colonials.

In the evening I made my way to what seemed to be the 'mecca' of all servicemen in the town, The Grand Hotel, where a dance was in progress. On entering the dance hall, I had my most pleasant surprise to date. Of some 300 or so people in the hall, only about a third were men, the remainder were all women ranging in ages from about 16 to 50. I soon became the centre of attraction, either as a novelty or a curiosity, and to tell the truth, I didn't really care which. I not only danced every dance, but was excused almost every dance by three or four different girls. The experience was so unique, and I was generally having such a good time, I made no attempt to analyse the reason. Why look a gift horse in the mouth? Why indeed?

Although the inhabitants of the nearby village of Hunmanby Moor were somewhat apprehensive of us recruits when we first arrived, by the time we were nearing the end of our training, a number of us had made friends among the locals, and were regular visitors to some of their homes. My particular friend was the village post mistress, a charming and very hospitable lady.

About this time Ernest, a couple of boys from another flight, and myself, decided it would be a good idea if we could organise a concert for the last week-end of our stay, and invite our village friends as a sort of thank you gesture. The camp commandant was delighted with the suggestion, and gave it his blessing. The camp cinema was put at our disposal to stage the event.

We were able to borrow props from an ENSA party who were entertaining troops in the area at the time. Many of the British officers and airmen with entertaining experience gave valuable

41

advice. A 'steel band' was improvised, using an old oil drum cut in half, spoons and forks, combs wrapped in tissue paper, and even bits of metal rods. I venture to suggest that these unsophisticated Yorkshire villagers were perhaps the very first English people to hear an authentic West Indian steel band at play.

For the event, I composed and read a monologue, sang a calypso, of which I wrote the lyrics, and Ernest was the principal character in a comedy sketch. There was also a song and dance act. At the end of the war, the lead singer of the song and dance act became a household name in Britain as leading vocalist with Geraldo, a nationally renowned dance band, who were regularly featured on the radio for many years. The entire venture was a huge success, and on the Monday following the concert, the commanding officer received a letter from the villagers, bearing some 50 or more signatures, stating that, 'of the thousands of recruits who had passed through the training centre, the West Indians were the best behaved, and had given the least cause for complaint'. What was more, an open invitation was extended to any member of that draft of recruits to visit their village when on leave, and enjoy all the civic amenities free of charge. In addition, the signatories were prepared to offer accommodation, free of charge, to any two recruits at any one time. This latter offer could be taken up by writing to the village post office.

As the day of our final passing-out parade drew nearer, rivalry between the flights became intense, and was reflected not only among us recruits, but also our instructors. On one occasion a particularly difficult manoeuvre was being perfected, but after an hour there were still members of the squad who were not up to the standard the flight sergeant thought necessary. This was taking place on the drill square and after all this time some of the recruits began to show unmistakable signs of weariness. To our relief we were marched off the square, for a rest as we thought. This was an illusion which was soon made plain. Instead we were marched to the road opposite the camp's sick bay. 'Do you know why we have come here?' asked the flight sergeant. 'Well, I'll tell you. So that anyone who collapses will not have far to go for medical attention.' He made his point and got the perfection he sought. It was therefore no more than everyone expected, when, on final passing-out parade, Flight Four won the much sought after title of 'Best Flight'. The surprise would have been, if we had failed to do so.

There was one other event of prime importance, morale wise, which took place during our last week at RAF Filey. Unknown to us the Air Ministry had been making a film of us from the day of our arrival at Liverpool, right up to a few days before our final passing-out, and this film was shown to us before we left Filey for our various destinations. Speaking for myself I can honestly say I felt very proud when I saw myself on film going through some of my military paces, knowing that the film was at that very time being shown in the West Indies. Although at times we felt that we were being pushed to the utmost limits of our endurance, in the final result, we were just as proud of our instructors, as I am sure they were of us.

We were now fully trained combatants, as far as fighting goes, but trade and operational training still lay ahead of us. I had volunteered as a wireless air gunner (WOP.A.G.) or flight engineer. But because the war was now in its final stages (just weeks before the Normandy landings), the need for men to be trained in these occupations no longer existed. Consequently, all of us, who had put in for air crew training for whatever category, were asked to remuster to ground staff activities. Ernest and myself, who had become very close friends, put in for a radar course, but unfortunately at the last moment I took ill and had to go into hospital, whilst the remainder of my colleagues went off on their respective training courses. As a result of this period of hospitalization, I not only lost contact with my former chalet mates, but was forced to settle for a clerical (general duties) career. The next time I saw Ernest Peart was on this holiday to Jamaica. By then he was a minister in Michael Manley's government. Needless to say we had a marvellous reunion at his home, where I had so much to drink, he had his chauffeur drive me home as protection from would-be muggers or foot pads.

CHAPTER 4. *Loving in Cornwall & First Footing in Scotland.*

Eventually, in September of 1944, I reported to the orderly room of No. 1 Overseas Air Despatch Unit (OADU), Portreath, Cornwall, near the north cliffs. The building, a pre-fabricated one, was situated just off the perimeter track. I handed my posting papers to the WAAF clerk at the counter, just inside the main entrance, and was told to wait while she disappeared with my orders into an inner office marked 'Adjutant'. Almost immediately I distinctly heard her say, 'he is black, and his papers state that he is a "Clerk General Duties". I wonder if he can read?' A male voice replied. 'That's interesting. Well, I had better have a word with him.' I think they must have forgotten how thin the ply-wood partition was, and that their voices would easily carry to where I was waiting. On hearing the last remark, I walked towards the entrance door, giving the impression when the airwoman returned, that I had been looking out the front door and could not therefore have heard the conversation that had just taken place.

Raising the flap at one end of the counter, and indicating the door from which she had just emerged, she said, 'the adjutant will see you now'. I thanked her, knocked firmly on the door she indicated, and in response to a voice saying, 'come in', I entered.

Sitting at a mahogany desk, with an in tray to his right, an out tray to his left and a filing cabinet up against the far wall, was a flight lieutenant. He had a large ginger coloured moustache (handle-bar type), which almost completely obscured his face from the tip of his nose to the end of his upper lip, and extending beyond the corners of his mouth. The effect was more comic than elegant. All this I took in with one sweeping glance.

'Sit down, airman', said handle-bars, indicating the chair facing him. The voice was well modulated and cultured. His eyes were hazel and he had a friendly, if somewhat bewildered smile. 'Welcome to Portreath, I am Flight Lieutenant Poppledown (I don't remember his real name), the adjutant. I see you are posted to No. I OADU. Would you like to tell me something about yourself? For a start, what part of the world are you from?' I replied that I was from Jamaica, and had volunteered as there was no conscription in the West Indies. (I wanted to make the point at once that I was here from choice.) 'I have been in England just over a year, having spent a month in the USA en route to Britain,' 'Did you enjoy your trip over?' 'Frankly no', I replied, 'although my short stay in America was very pleasant.' 'Yes, the Americans are very hospitable, and they are doing a grand job in the war. If only they did not brag so damned much.'

It was obvious to me that this aspect of the American character rankled with him. The impression was that, the adjutant, whilst not exactly reticent himself, was hardly the type who indulged in boastfulness. 'We are a happy crew here', he continued, 'we do air sea rescue work. The object of the exercise is to try to spot any of our chaps that may have had to ditch in the drink, radio their position to our Launch Rescue Unit, and to the navy, who then fish them out. Things tend to get hectic at times, but we somehow manage to cope. (The typical British understatement.) You of course will be concerned with the despatch of aircraft and aircrew to overseas units.'

Bearing in mind the conversation I had overheard, I was prepared for an entirely different sort of interview. Clearly, he was making rapid mental readjustments of his opinion of me, as I could almost see his brain ticking over in an attempt to assess and docket me as neatly as the papers in the open file lying on his desk.

The adjutant's voice broke in on my thoughts. 'I will not keep you any longer. When you go out into the corridor, turn right and enter the second door on your left. That will be the orderly room proper. The sergeant-in-charge will give you your arrival forms and booking-in instructions. Once you have eaten and freshened up, I want you to return here so that I can take you to see the station commander, who likes to meet and welcome all new arrivals personally.'

The camp was sited on a plateau overlooking the sea, with a sheer drop of several hundred feet. Immediately below the cliffs, ran a ribbon of road, which wound itself along the beach, connecting with the major road to Penzance on the left, and

Redruth and Exeter to the right. The base was a fairly large one with a couple of Fighter-Bombers and one Spitfire squadron. The Spitfires were manned by Polish airmen, who had escaped to Britain to continue the struggle against the common enemy. The Fighter-Bomber squadrons were manned by mixed crews, mostly Commonwealth volunteers, and a few Free-French airmen.

My duties at No. I OADU were pretty straightforward. At this stage of the war our function was principally the transfer of aircraft and their crews from one theatre of operations to another as situations developed. After about a fortnight at Portreath, I had my first 48 hours pass out of camp, and on the afternoon of the first day I went to Redruth, where I had tea and took in a cinema show. Shortly after the film started, I became vaguely aware of someone sitting down in the seat immediately to my left. Some little while after this I lit myself a cigarette. The new arrival also got out a cigarette, and fished around in her hand bag unsuccessfully, then leaned across and asked for a light. In the light of the match, I noticed that she was rather good looking, a bit on the plump side, and fortyish. She thanked me, rather profusely I thought, and returned to concentrate on the film.

At the interval she again asked for a light, and followed this up by asking what part of the world I was from, and where I was stationed. By the time the lights went out again for the main feature, I knew her name (let's say it was Daisy), that she lived alone a couple of miles from our present position, she was a munitions worker, and she had not seen her husband, who was overseas, for more than two years.

She invited me to take tea with her after the show but, to avoid gossip, she asked that we should not leave the cinema together. Instead, I should leave ten minutes before her and wait for her about a mile along the road. What do you know? I was being picked up, and to say I was delighted would be putting it mildly.

To those of my readers who may be tempted to pass judgement at this late date, I would say don't. War not only destroys buildings and kills human beings, it also decimates moral values. Although the permissive society of today had not yet arrived, the strain of nearly five years of war had produced a

46

fatalistic frame of mind which dictated that one should enjoy today for all its worth, as there may be no tomorrow. Women, particularly married women who had lost their men, or had not seen them for years on end, had sexual desires which could not be denied indefinitely. By this I am not implying that *all* married women were unfaithful to their spouses during the war, only that some, for one reason or another, succumbed to the pressures and sought satisfaction for their natural needs, and it would be quite wrong to lightly condemn those that fell by the wayside as being morally degenerate.

To get back to my encounter with Daisy. We met as arranged, and I spent that night, and many more, so many more, with her during my stay at Portreath. Close as the relationship was, there was never any question of permanency between us. There was a perfectly clear understanding that should her husband suddenly return, I would immediately fade out of her life, no recriminations, and no regrets. When subsequently I met and fell in love with a girl who was holidaying with a relation near my camp, Daisy was the first person to know, but it made not the slightest difference to our affair of convenience. In the years following my departure from Cornwall I have often wondered if, and hoped that her husband survived the war to return to her.

About two months after meeting Daisy, I was walking up to the top of the cliffs one afternoon with the intention of enjoying the panoramic view of the villages that lay nestled at its base, and to watch the sea breakers smashing against the cliff walls. Suddenly it started raining quite heavily, as often happens in this part of Cornwall. At about the same time I spotted a young lady pushing a bicycle up the hill towards me. I could see she was having some difficulty coping with the cycle on the, by now, very slippery surface of the hill. With no other thought in mind but to help a lady in difficulty, I retraced my steps and offered to push the cycle up the hill for her. She gladly accepted, and surrendered the offending bicycle to my charge. As we walked on I noticed that she was ash-blonde, with eyes of azure blue, which seemed to dance with merriment when she smiled, as she was now doing, and my heart skipped a beat. In a voice that sounded like music to my smitten ears, she asked if I was from the RAF camp at Portreath? (I was of course in uniform.) I replied that I was, and asked if she lived in the area? 'No', she replied, 'I am

47

visiting my aunt who lives at Pengegon on the other side of these cliffs. This is my first visit to Cornwall, and, like you, I wanted to see the view from the top, which I am told is well worth the effort. Now however, it is quite impossible to see anything because of the rain clouds.' We had by now reached the top, and she suggested that if we took a path to our right between some disused tin mines, she thought it might bring us to the aunt's house, or near it, in about 15 minutes, long before I could possibly reach my camp. 'Why not come back with me for a cup of tea and a dry-out in front of the fire? I am sure aunty won't mind. She would want to thank you for helping me anyway.' I readily accepted, and we set off across the fields for her aunt's home.

After about three quarters of an hour, it became plain we had lost our way. Unfortunately there were quite a number of disused mines in the area, and they all looked alike. Whilst trying to find a path that would take us somewhere near our destination, I told her of my home in Jamaica, and how I came to be in the air force. She in turn told me her name was Olive, she lived with her widowed mother in a small village just outside Wolverhampton, and that she played the piano as a member of an ENSA Concert Party, who toured the county entertaining servicemen. Eventually we came out onto a road a mile or so from her home. By then we were very wet, but unusually cheerful under the circumstances. In fact we were practically in tears laughing at ourselves. By the time we got to the house we were positively firm friends.

Tea at aunty's was a tremendous success. Olive played the piano and sang. Not to be outdone, I also sang a calypso, while aunty passed bantering judgement on our performances. From that evening on, until her departure for Wolverhampton at the end of her holiday, we met almost daily and had many a climb to the top of the cliffs. Long before her departure we both knew we were falling in love, and so did aunty, who pleaded a prior engagement, so that she did not have to accompany us to the station. On the platform, we embraced, kissed, and promised to write daily. It was then, for the first time, on recalling that I was due to visit Daisy that night that I had a distinct feeling of guilt, nay revulsion, at the thought of going to bed with her so soon after saying farewell to the girl I loved, and, yes, why not admit it, hoped to marry. Instead of going to Daisy I caught the next bus back to camp.

Although I continued to see her after this, but less frequently, I made quite sure she knew of my love for Olive, and, to do her justice, she wished me every success in the pursuit of my dreams. For the next six months Olive and I corresponded regularly, and met occasionally when I could get a few days leave. Because of the distance I would have to travel from Portreath to Wolverhampton, we compromised and met half way, usually in London. All the time our love was growing and becoming more impatient of enforced separation. Then to my great delight I was posted to No. 8 PFF (Pathfinder Force) near Huntingdon, attached to the Lancaster Servicing Section. This move, once and for all put an end to my affair with Daisy who had become a habit with me, which I could no more resist than an addict his drug. Yet, when the time came for me to leave Portreath there were no regrets for the past, and no promises for the future. We had filled a temporary need in each other, and knew it could never be anything more than just that.

Shortly after joining 8 PFF, I sustained serious injuries including a perforated diaphragm, when caught up in a doodle bug raid on my way back from a weekend visit to London, and was admitted to the RAF hospital Ely in Cambridgeshire. As soon as Olive learnt of my accident and hospitalization, she travelled down to Ely, staying at a small boarding house near the hospital, in order to be near me. Because of rehearsal commitments for a forthcoming concert with her ENSA group, she could only stay in Ely for three days. Three blissfully happy days for me, even in hospital, because she visited me twice daily thereby psychologically, if not physically, speeding up my eventual recovery. Before leaving for home she made me promise I would spend any convalescent leave I may get with her and her mother, if the RAF would allow it. Before this was possible, however, her mother had to satisfy the hospital's chief medical officer of her ability not only to provide the necessary care I would need, but suitable transportation from the railway station at Wolverhampton to her home at Oxley, as I was still too weak to cope with public transport.

This assurance having been given, some three weeks after Olive's return to Oxley from Ely, I was conveyed by ambulance

49

to the station at Ely, bound for the Drinkwater's home on three weeks convalescence. On arrival at Wolverhampton, Olive was there with a taxi ready to convey me to her mother's house. The drive from the station to her home gave us a few precious moments together before coming under the maternal gaze. This being the first time I would be meeting her mother, Olive felt she had to brief me on what to expect.

Mrs Drinkwater received me with open arms and commiserations for my present indisposition. She also said she considered it a privilege to be able to accommodate me during my convalescence as it was very little after the sacrifice I had made in leaving my home thousands of miles across the world, to come and help to defend their homes and way of life. For the next two weeks I enjoyed the unrivalled hospitality of Olive and her mother. Mrs Drinkwater did everything that was humanly possible for my material comfort, whilst Olive administered to my emotional needs.

At the end of a fortnight, predictably I suppose, I proposed and Olive accepted. But the path of true love was not destined to run smoothly on this occasion. In fiction it is easy for the author to so decree, but in real life it rarely is ever that easy. When the news was broken to Mrs Drinkwater she flatly refused to countenance the idea. For the first time I was to have a real taste of 'colour prejudice' and English hypocrisy. Her objection to the union went something like this: 'You are a very fine young man, doing a grand job in the air force, and I like you very much as a person, but you cannot be really serious in wanting to marry my daughter. You are not really in love, just infatuated. You would never be really happy, your backgrounds are so very different. I am not saying that if you were born in this country, and accustomed to the same things, it might not have been different. But in England it just is not "the done thing".' Note the care she took not to mention my colour even once, yet, there cannot be the slightest doubt that her objections were based solely on the colour of my skin.

During these exchanges between her mother and myself, Olive kept a discreet silence. Now, however, she told her mother firmly that she was old enough (23 years) to make up her own mind as to who was, or was not, a suitable person for her to marry. Moreover, she loved me and had every intention of marrying me, with or without her consent, although she would much prefer to have her blessing.

After this it was obvious I could no longer remain in the house, especially as Mrs Drinkwater further accused me of abusing her hospitality by making undue advances to her daughter. This accusation was so ludicrous that I did not feel it necessary to point out to her the fact that her daughter and myself had been corresponding and meeting regularly with her full knowledge. Olive had visited me in hospital with her knowledge and consent, and finally, *she herself* had endorsed my invitation to her home by confirming to the RAF medical officer that she agreed to the visit and would provide transportation to her home and the necessary medical care my condition required.

The very next day I said a polite, but decidedly frigid farewell to Olive's mother. In the taxi on the way to the station, Olive again reaffirmed her love for me and determination to follow the dictates of her heart. The remaining few days of my convalescence were spent in London, even though I had to run the gauntlet of the military police as my leave pass was made out for the Wolverhampton area and, as such, I had no right to be in London.

Shortly after returning to my unit I had a communication from Olive telling me that she had applied for, and been accepted as a trainee youth leader with the Young Women's Christian Association (YWCA) and would be reporting to their training college at Kidderpore Gardens, Hampstead, London, in a month's time. In other words, she was leaving home. Although I regretted the rift that made this necessary, I would be less than honest if I said I was not delighted that she had taken her stand on the side of our continued relationship.

During the first few months of her training we saw quite a lot of each other as I had permission from the Air Ministry to take part in the BBC's 'Hands Across the Atlantic' radio broadcast from their studio at 200 Oxford Street, and had to make a number of visits to the studio for rehearsals. Olive invariably accompanied me on these visits, but unfortunately, when the actual broadcast went out she was unable to be present. In order to compensate, I obtained tickets from the BBC for us to attend a live Richard Tauber broadcast from the Paris Cinema. This was rather a feather in my cap, in that, in spite of Olive's connection with the ENSA Group, it was through me that she was first able to witness a 'live radio broadcast'.

Olive had apparently spoken to her principals at the college about me and the broadcast, because she was asked to try and get me to give the Empire Day lecture on the 24th May, 1945. This I agreed to do assuming I got Air Ministry approval. This was given, and in due course I delivered a lecture on 'West Indian Dress and Customs'. On the day following this event we took the opportunity of my presence in London to select Olive's engagement ring from a firm of jewellers at Oxford Circus. The question of the timing of our marriage was occupying our thoughts very much. Olive felt we ought to wait until she had completed her two years training and I had my discharge from the air force. This I reluctantly agreed to, although I would have preferred a shorter period of engagement.

Shortly after the college authorities learnt of our engagement, we both received an invitation to tea from Lady Proctor, chairman of Forces Work YWCA, at her Baker Street flat, which we naturally accepted. Lady Proctor was in every respect a 'lady', very courteous and charming, but it was obvious to me that I was being vetted for my suitability. However, apart from pointing out the difficulties we were bound to encounter in the prevailing attitude to mixed marriages, she managed to maintain a completely non-committal stance. Subsequent developments, however, have given me cause to question her neutrality in the matter.

For the next six months Olive was sent to a number of clubs for short periods to gain 'field' experience. The first of these was the Pilgrim House Club, Bow Road, East London, where I was also invited to address the members. She next went to the Reading Club, Berks, where I again addressed a mixed gathering of YWCA and YMCA members. I had by now broadened my theme and was in some considerable demand lecturing on 'West Indian History and Cultural Development'. My next lecture on this subject was to the Cambridge University branch of The Royal Empire Society. Olive and myself had gone to Cambridge for this event on the eve of my lecture, and incidentally, the very day the end of the war in Europe was announced (VE Day).

It is almost impossible for me to adequately describe here,

after all these years, the incredible scenes of joy and sheer abandonment which took place in Cambridge that day and night. Complete strangers would hug and kiss you in the streets, shops and parks. There was dancing in the streets, and bonfires everywhere. In a park near the university I saw servicemen and officers take off their tunics and throw them on a massive bonfire. Couples were unashamedly making love on the grass with very little attempt to disguise their actions. What was more startling was the fact that no one seemed to be paying them much attention, or evinced any surprise. At any rate, that's how it seemed to me at the time.

Just about this time Bomber Command was organising flying tours over Germany for members of ground staff, giving us an opportunity to see for ourselves the damage which the air crews had inflicted on the enemy, aided by the support provided by the men and women on the ground a sort of thank you 'Cooks Tour'. In fact we did dub them Cooks Tours. Shortly after my return from Cambridge, I applied to be included on one and eventually made the trip in a Lancaster bomber. Whilst flying over Cologne I took a picture, with an ordinary Baby Browning camera from the rear turret of the Lancaster, of the remains of the famous cathedral with its celebrated twin spires the only thing still intact. I also took a picture from the same position of the burnt out remains of the Krupps munitions factory while flying over Essen.

An interesting side light to this episode is that some 30 years later my eldest daughter won a scholarship while attending university to study drama in Germany, and was able to visit those sites, thereby in a way identifying herself with my war exploits.

One other event of particular interest took place during my period at RAF Wyton. Camp gossip had it that the dance halls of Peterborough were the place to be if one was looking for some female company and a bit of excitement at the weekend. What it did not say was that certain halls were virtually occupied by servicemen of one or two nationalities, and it was unwise to stray into one of these on one's own. One Saturday night I decided to give Peterborough a whirl. With no clear idea of which hall to attend, when I saw a sign which read 'Drill Hall Dancing, All Servicemen Welcome', I dived in. To my complete surprise practically all the servicemen present were either American airmen (white), or Canadian parachutists, with no more than half a dozen British Tommies, and not a single member of the RAF. What is more, I was the only black face in sight.

In those days I was as fearless as they come, and thought, here I am, here I stay. It did not take me long to sort out a likely partner for the night. A saucy looking brunette of five foot nothing caught my eye and I moved in. Dorothy may not have had the face of Marilyn Monroe but she could surely give the famous star a run for her money in shape and wiggle of walk. And what a jitterbugger she was! I was myself no mean mover on the dance floor; even today at 60 years plus I can still hold my own against young uns' half my age at a disco.

We had been dancing together for about half-an-hour, when I was tapped on the shoulder during a dance by an American airman. This particular dance was not an 'excuse me', so I ignored the signal and continued my dancing girations. This airman was not prepared to be ignored by a mere negro, he continued his tapping until I was forced to tell him to 'piss off'. His reply to this was the statement that 'where I come from we do things to niggers who play around with white women'. 'Your hard luck chum, this is England, not America.' Without further ado he slapped me very hard across the face. He was a good six foot and well built. In a flash I realised I had bitten off more than I could possibly chew. My only chance lay in some element of surprise, so I pretended to back off. This had the effect of momentarily putting him off his guard and, quick as a flash, I dived at his feet, grabbed the bottom of his trouser legs and yanked upwards with all my strength, just as quickly he was laying on his back in the middle of the dance floor.

I was just about to put the boot in to make sure he did not get up, when I was held from behind by one of the Canadians. 'You do not kick a man when he is down, not even a yankey bastard.' By now about three or four of my opponent's friends had joined him, and it was obvious they were going to sort me out. My Canadian acquaintance put himself between them and me and shepherded me over to where the rest of his friends were gathered. 'Look airman, we do not like these yanks any more than you do, so I suggest that my friends and I escort you to your bus stop or railway station straight away, otherwise they'll be waiting for you outside when you leave here.' Although it was still quite early, I decided discretion was the better part of valour, and accepted the offer.

Sad to say I have never again visited Peterborough since that Saturday night some 37 or 38 years ago. It is my intention to remedy that in the not very distant future. If for no other reason but to visit its magnificent cathedral.

Later that year Olive was sent to a club in Cardiff, Wales, and I was posted to an RAF maintenance unit in Carluke, Scotland. I was attached to the education section, which was one of the new educational vocation training centres (EVT) set up to prepare airmen due for early release, for re-entry to civilian life. Although I have no proof of outside interference, the timing of our individual postings was too fortuitous to be lightly dismissed as coincidence. Scotland-Wales; if this was a planned move to keep us apart, as I suspected, it was certainly achieving its objective. Every request of mine for a posting back to England was turned down by the powers-that-be. What is more, her letters were taking an extraordinary length of time to reach me if they did at all. Those that did, were being censored although the war had ended some months now.

It is difficult for me to say, with any accuracy, what precisely was Olive's reaction to our enforced separation. I hope I am not doing her an injustice when I say I started to detect a cooling off in the tone of her letters that were now reaching me. In the end the romance, that had promised so much, just fizzled out and died. I have often wondered if Olive did eventually marry? If she did, I sincerely hope she had better luck than I had in my first marriage. Is it too much to ask if she ever remembers a recalcitrant bicycle and a Jamaican airman in the rain on the north cliffs of Cornwall?

My new camp, which was about 18 miles from Glasgow, was by any standard a 'cushy' posting in normal circumstances. Fortunately for me, the educaton officer was also the motor transport officer (MTO), and since his duties required his presence abroad for long periods, organising the return of damaged and no longer required aircraft and vehicles to the UK, I had a pretty free hand in the education section. 'When the cat's away, the mice will play.'

For airmen visiting Glasgow from RAF Carluke, the 9.30 pm

bus was the last through-one back to camp. If it was missed, one could only get as far as Wishaw, where a local connection had to be caught for the remainder of the journey. On one such occasion, I was waiting at the bus stop in Wishaw when a couple approached me and enquired if I was waiting for the bus to Carluke? I replied that I was, and was told that I had the best part of another hour to wait. This being a Sunday, the buses ran only half as frequently as they did on week days. 'You seem frozen', they continued (it was a bitterly cold night in early December), 'would you care to come home with us for a cup of tea? We will make sure that you get back in good time for your bus to camp.' How could one refuse such spontaneous hospitality? And on a freezing cold night at that. It would have been absolutely churlish to do so. I therefore accepted the invitation with alacrity, and accompanied them to their home a short distance away.

Once tea was out of the way, Mr & Mrs Transtow (that is not their real name) insisted on my staying for a demonstration of their daughter's musical talents, which the would-be musician was only too anxious to display. I of course had no alternative but to accept, and resigned myself to the prospect of half-an-hour's boredom. After flicking her fingers along the keyboard, she launched herself into what can only truthfully be described as a magnificent recital of Chopin's nocturne. Long before she was finished, I was sitting on the edge of my chair absolutely spellbound by the sheer beauty of her playing. Considering that, according to her parents, she had had no really serious classical training, it was, to say the least, an amazing performance.

During the course of the evening I discovered that my host and his brother-in-law were both keen bridge players. When I informed him that I also played, he was delighted and insisted that whenever possible I should join them to make up a foursome. This invitation I had no difficulty in accepting as my game was getting rusty through lack of practice. This unique encounter was to provide me for the remainder of my stay in Scotland with many hours of intellectual stimulation, and pure unadulterated Scots hospitality.

The foursome for bridge, which was played every Thursday night, consisted of Mr and Mrs Transtow, his brother-in-law and myself. For the remainder of my stay in Scotland these two families took turns at entertaining me. When it was not bridge, it would be a whist drive at the Catholic church hall in Hamilton, or a football game in Hamilton or Glasgow, and on one occasion I even attended a 'Burns Supper' and ate my regulation portion of haggis.

The most important event in the Scottish calendar is Christmas and New Year, particularly New Year or 'Hogmanay' when the Scots really let their hair down. At my first Hogmanay I was told, and I repeat 'told', not asked, that I would be the 'first footer' for my Wishaw friends. In Scotland, tradition, or superstition, it matters not which, decrees that if the first person to enter the house on New Year's Day is dark, it augers well for the whole of the ensuing year. A dark person for that purpose is anyone with dark hair. To have someone who not only had dark hair, but was also naturally dark skinned, was unique. This happy coincidence they considered could not help but bring good fortune for the rest of the year.

Another tradition, connected with Hogmanay, is that everyone who enters the house on New Year's Day should bring a present. I understand that in the mining areas of England this is also the custom. But whereas in England it's a lump of coal which is taken into the house, in Scotland it is more often than not a bottle of whisky. This practice stems from the belief that it will ensure the house will never be short of provisions for the rest of the year.

In Scotland every member of the house party is expected to have a drink from the bottle of every other guest. If the party numbers nigh on a score of guests, as is usually the case, it needs no great stretch of the imagination to understand why Hogmanay is such a merry affair. I broke the whisky tradition in that my bottle was not whisky but Jamaica Rum saved from my Mother's Christmas parcel to me. This as it turned out was a very welcome innovation. There was one jarring note, however, which concerned a guest who thought he was capable of drinking any kind of spirit 'neat'. I warned him that this was not the emasculated drink obtained in the pubs at the time, masquerading under the guise of Jamaica Rum, but the genuine overproof spirit, which meant it was well over 100% proof. He nevertheless poured himself a good half a tumbler of rum and downed it neat. Well, I ask you? Even I, who was brought up with rum as my national drink, would not have been so foolhardy. Within a very short time, he was not just being violently sick, he was vomiting blood. This apart, everyone had a right royal time. After a generous supply of whiskies and a couple of rums, I was singing Scottish folk songs and dancing the eightsome reel like any seasoned native.

E.M. Noble in 1942, Kingston, Jamaica

E.M. Noble with a friend at Doctor's Cave, Montego Bay, about 1940

The parish church in Port Maria, where E.M. Noble sang in the choir

E.M. Noble on a trip to Jamaica, 1947; right: *swimming at Port Maria Bay*

E.M. Noble with friends standing by the Lancaster bomber in which he made a trip over Germany. The photo was taken at RAF Wyton, Hunts.

E.M. Noble with friends (above) *at the War Graves Commission, RAF Stanmore, 1949*

E.M. Noble with fellow officers (above) and at a picnic (below) at Gunthorpe, near Nottingham, 12 Group Fighter Command Headquarters

Bob Smith and E.M. Noble by the grave of the unknown warrior under the Arc de Triomphe, Paris, 1951

E.M. Noble with his daughters in 1965 (left) and with his dog Sandy in 1979 (right)

E.M. Noble with members of the Jack Watts and District Tenants' Association Youth Club, which he founded and ran, at their 1982 Christmas Party (above); and with his wife at a tea dance in Benidorm (below)

E.M. Noble's mother in Port Maria, Jamaica, 1966

CHAPTER 5. *A Fight in Manchester.*

After a very happy and enjoyable 18 months in Scotland I was posted to another maintenance unit, RAF Handforth, near Stockport in Cheshire. After Scotland this little corner of England was something of an anticlimax. Handforth was within easy reach of Stockport and Manchester, so naturally I tended to gravitate to these two centres for my social activities. Stockport on weekday nights, it being only a short bus ride away, and Manchester at the weekends.

There were four of us West Indians stationed at RAF Handforth, three of us Jamaicans and one Trinidadian. Whenever we went to Stockport we invariably went to the same public house which was situated at the top of some steps above the local bus station. Unfortunately after all these years I just cannot recall the name of the pub. The other two Jamaicans were members of the same dance band back in Jamaica, one played the saxophone and the other drums. The saxophonist's name was Miller, and the pub's customers soon dubbed him Glen Miller after the popular American band leader of that name, who had earlier lost his life on a flight from England to France to entertain American troops. The third member of the quartet played the piano and I provided the vocals.

For the duration of our stay at RAF Handforth, whenever we went to that pub in Stockport we provided the night's entertainment. We would regale its customers with Jamaican calypsos and mentos, many of the lyrics written by myself. We also did request numbers of popular ditties of the day. Our only reward, apart from personal enjoyment, was the fact that we never had to pay for our own drinks, and we all had very good appetites.

Although Manchester had more to offer in the form of entertainment, it was the least lovable of the two for me. The scenery was so depressing and the weather generally so atrocious, they were not calculated to endear the place to any but the most partisan. It seemed to me at the time that Manchester must surely be the gloomiest industrial city in England.

The good fortune I had enjoyed up until now, of making friends with people of similar tastes and outlook, suddenly deserted me. I no longer had any common meeting ground with the vast majority of people I encountered in Manchester. If anything, they seemed to resent me for no better reason than the colour of my skin. Manchester was to make me painfully aware of a most unpleasant truth. 'Colour prejudice' is far more rife among ordinary working people than it is among the middle and upper middle classes.

Perhaps it was not so much that this latter group were that less prejudiced, but they were probably better able to conceal it. They certainly did not deliberately flout it at every opportunity. Whereas with the other group there was no such restraint. Their attitude seemed to be, 'since we are nobodies we must find someone or some group, such as Jews or Blacks, on whom to vent our frustrations and inadequacies and give a boost to our ego'. Be that as it may, life was certainly made difficult for me during this period. For example, like most servicemen when away from camp, I liked to go dancing or to the pub for a drink. In Manchester, in contrast to London, Edinburgh or Glasgow, in a pub no one spoke to me, and if I tried to make conversation they would either completely ignore me, or move away to another part of the bar. If I went to the counter for service the bar maid, or man, would elect to ignore my presence and repeated requests for a drink, until everyone else had been served, even those who came well after me.

Without saying a word they made it abundantly clear I was not welcome, uniform or no uniform. At local dance halls I often remained all night without being able to get a dance. On the rare occasions when a girl was brave enough to have a dance with me, a knot of her friends and acquaintances would surround her from then on, and persuade her not to repeat the performance. The exception was the excellent Nuffield Centre at the Deans Gate end of the city. The centre invited approved young ladies two or three times per week to act as dancing partners to the servicemen who attended the centre.

At the end of one of my visits to the centre, I was escorting my night's dancing partner to her bus stop. On the way we passed a public house whose clientele were just leaving for the night. On seeing us, a man, accompanied by two young women, detached himself from the rest of the people leaving the pub and started to follow us, keeping up a running commentary about 'niggers' who went out with white girls. The stranger was repeatedly told by his two companions to 'leave well alone as we were doing no harm to anyone'. My lady friend advised me to ignore his remarks and pretend I did not hear them. The stranger was so close behind us, he overheard what was said. That was too much for him it would seem. He now addressed his remarks directly to her, calling her a slut and 'nigger lover'. At this latest provocation I completely lost my patience and self-control. I turned, and hit our tormentor with a vicious left hook, and followed it up with a right cross. He fell to the ground, and was assisted to his feet by his two women friends.

We did not wait for his reaction, but continued our journey. We were not to be left in peace however. He was determined to avenge, if he could, the blow to his pride. He was approaching again with threats of what he was going to do to the black so-and-so. I was by now a very angry airman, ready for any move he might make. When he caught up with us again, I turned to face him, determined to settle this hassle once and for all. This time he led first, I easily avoided the blow, at the same time I uppercut him, and followed with a cluster of rights and lefts to head and body. He fell as if pole-axed, and remained still.

For an agonising moment I thought I had done him serious harm, but he was only winded. He got to his feet somewhat unsteadily. By now a crowd had gathered, and a policeman materialised as if from nowhere. The constable was in no mood for explanations from me. He was insisting that I accompany him to the station, in spite of the protestations of my lady friend. At this stage of the proceedings the two women companions of the stranger, pressed their way to the front and introduced themselves as the wife and sister of the victim. They then informed the constable that their companion was entirely to blame for what had taken place. He had had too much to drink and was in a quarrelsome mood even before they left the pub. This was followed by a truc and accurate account of all that had taken place.

With this information coming from so unimpeachable a source, this particular limb of the law had no choice but to let me go my way. A satisfactory ending to a most unpleasant occurrence.

61

Nevertheless, it left a rather nasty taste in the mouth. Note also that no attempt was made to charge, or even warn the culprit about his behaviour. An excess of alcohol is never in itself the cause of prejudice, it is merely the spur, or, if you prefer, the false courage that brings those latent emotions to the surface.

It should not be inferred from the foregoing observations that I found nothing to admire in either the people or their institutions. On the contrary, as the reader is already aware, football and cricket are the sporting loves of my life, and in Manchester I had ample opportunity to indulge them as a spectator. It is, I think, generally accepted that Lancashire league cricket provides some of the most attractive and competitive cricket anywhere in the country. Also, at that time, it was the repository for such overseas stalwarts of the game as George Headley of Jamaica and Learie Constantine of Trinidad, to name but two. It is for this reason, more than any other, that I remain mystified to this day by the unsporting treatment meted out to me in Manchester, which was so contrary to the character of a cricket loving community.

Following on my BBC broadcast from London, I was invited to do a second from the Manchester studios, and, as a direct consequence of this latter, was asked to address the joint YWCA/YMCA youth club in the town of Blackburn. I accepted the invitation on condition that it be kept quiet and informal as I did not intend to seek Air Ministry or my commanding officer's permission to undertake it. (I was still smarting over my posting to Scotland which I was convinced led to my broken romance.) The absence of official permission meant that I had to be back in camp before 'colour hoisting parade' the following morning. I kept the appointment in due course and departed Blackburn, after my address, at 10.30 p.m. on the last bus for Preston, where I intended connecting with the 'long distance coach' from London to Morecombe, which would have put me down within a couple miles of my camp.

Imagine my consternation, when I got to Preston and went to purchase my ticket, to discover I had lost my wallet? I felt reasonably certain it had not been stolen, but lost. This was subsequently confirmed by the club official when it was returned to me some days later. Apparently I had dropped it in the toilet and a club member handed it in some time after my departure. The loss of my wallet presented me with an acute dilemma. How to get back to camp before first parade, without money, and the only available transport already gone. I knew there was an all-night WVS canteen in Preston, not far from the bus station, so I went there, told the lady-in-charge of my predicament, and asked if she could help.

Sure enough the WVS could and would help. She said she had a car of rather ancient vintage (her words), and was allowed sufficient petrol to go about her WVS work. As soon as her relief arrived at 5am she would drive me to camp herself; which indeed she did. About a week later I paid another visit to the canteen in order to thank her in a very practical manner, my benefactress was not on duty, but I learnt that that kind lady by driving me to camp had used up all her petrol allowance for the rest of the month and had to use public transport or walk to go about her charitable work. This event may not have changed my opinions of Manchester, but it surely restored my faith in some of the citizens of Lancashire.

By early 1947, discharge or repatriation of West Indian servicemen had begun, and I had to decide whether to take my discharge here in England or await repatriation back to Jamaica. Since it was still my ambition to pursue a legal career, I decided to take my discharge here as the best means of eventually achieving that ambition. Before this came about, however, I was posted to the RAF Polish Resettlement Camp at Melton Mowbray, Leicestershire. The only lasting memory I have of this particular camp is the nightmare of trying to spell accurately the names of the Polish officers, men and their families, when I had to prepare their documents for entry into civilian life, and the 'Sunday night dances' on camp.

There were some very pretty girls and wives among the Polish families, who were not averse to a bit of necking with the RAF personnel on camp. (The girls that is, not the wives.) This, however, could prove a very hazardous exercise as the Polish men were extremely jealous and protective of their women. I did feel at the time that this contrasted strangely with their own ram-like activities among the local girls around Melton and Leicester.

Later that year my discharge came through, and I used my end-of-emergency leave to pay a quick visit to my parents in

Jamaica, as I had no idea how long I would be in England or how long before I would be able to afford a trip home, once I had left the Air Force. There is nothing memorable to recall about that leave except the fact that I was overjoyed to see my family again, especially my grandmother. There were a number of house parties given by my close friends and relations in my honour, but I somehow never really got into the old spirit of fun. I think I had grown up and become more concerned about the future and where I was eventually headed, rather than the mere pursuit of immediate pleasure.

I did however make one business decision, I declined the offer of a plot of land which all returning servicemen were entitled to. I returned to England in the winter of that same year and immediately set about getting a job. I fondly thought that with my excellent service record and above average intelligence, this would present no problems, especially as industry was crying out for men of intelligence. I soon discovered however that the open invitation from the business world to all returning servicemen did not include black ex-servicemen. I answered scores of advertisements, had numerous interviews, but the result was always the same. As soon as I presented myself and they saw that I was black, the post would mysteriously just have been filled, or 'I would be informed in due course', but I never heard from them again, even to say I was unsuccessful. On other occasions I would be told they had decided to fill the post by internal promotion (that was whenever the job was of a senior grading), but it was too late to stop the advertisement.

One interview in particular stands out in my memory. I had answered an advertisement from a company, who manufactured a leading brand of typewriters (ironically the same brand as the one I am now using to write this memoir), for a senior clerk to take over the correspondence department at their West End offices. Applicants were asked to give a brief outline of their qualifications and experience in this type of work. On the strength of my replies, I was asked to call on the personnel officer for an interview. On arrival at reception, in spite of presenting my letter of appointment, the receptionist insisted there must be some mistake. When I angrily told her there was no mistake and demanded to see the personnel officer, she asked me to wait, and went off herself to acquaint him of not only my presence, but presumably my colour as well.

When she returned with the P.O. he conducted me to his office and went through the following charade. 'I am sorry you have been put to the inconvenience of this journey Mr Noble. The advertisement should have read, "of a junior clerk", but owing to typing error the newspaper had "senior clerk", and that is what our receptionist meant when she insisted that there must have been a mistake. I am quite sure from your qualifications and service record you would make a very valuable addition to our staff. Unfortunately, the salary we are able to offer for this post would not be enough for you to live on.'

I had had so much of this phoney type of excuse in the past, I decided to call his bluff. I replied (untruthfully) that I had some private means and was therefore quite prepared to accept a modest salary as I had to start somewhere to gain experience, in the firm conviction that I would be able to work my way up the salary scale by merit in the usual way. His reply to this was: 'Well, that's a reasonable request, but the final decision does not rest solely with me. If you care to wait here, I will consult my colleagues and let you know in a few minutes. You may smoke if you wish while waiting.'

He was away for much longer than I expected, more than half an hour. On his return he apologised for the length of his stay, and explained that the firm had no objection to employing me on the terms I suggested, but as I would be the very first black person to be engaged by them, his colleagues and himself felt obliged to consult those members of staff with whom I would have to work. 'Unfortunately, they flatly refuse to work with you. Whilst I personally deplore their attitude, I am afraid we have no choice but to turn down your offer. We could of course defy them and employ you anyway, but this would only land us with a strike on our hands, and we just cannot afford that. The interest of the company must take priority over that of any individual employee. Again I must apologise for the inconvenience we have caused you. We will of course reimburse your fares for the journey to attend this interview.'

I could hardly believe my ears. When it was a question of risking my life, fighting for this country, the colour of my skin was irrelevant, now that the war was over it was a different ball game altogether. I was so livid I told him exactly what I thought

of his lame excuses and what he could do with his offer to
reimburse my fares and, believe me when I tell you, it was
unprintable.

In childhood innocence I lent ears to historians and patriots
who decreed:

Be proud of your native land so rich and free,
bequeathed by men of deeds brave and bold,
who tamed the seas and dug the earth for gold.

But with broken shoes, patched up clothes, black skin and kinky
      hair,
I grew to manly strength of sinew; whilst in office,
      factory and farm,
I watched helpless as palefaced countrymen its bounties on
      others bestowed.

Yet, when mighty enemies would our fair land enslave,
      black of face though I be, my arms were welcomed for the
      ensuing fight,
As with spirit and determination we repulsed that hated enemy
      from our shores.

Having discharged my duty to King and Country with valour,
I marched home proudly to the sound of bells acclamour.
The fight now ended, the enemy defeated, I dared to hope the
      former pattern of things would not be repeated.

But alas my only reward, sanctimonious excuses,
closed doors, unanswered applications, a burning cross,
the chalked up slogan 'BLACKS GO HOME', in God's name
if this is not, where then is my home?

Brave comrades of yesteryear, with short-lived memories of
      today,
confound me with their baseless claim to integrity,
as they flounder in highflown, but cynical verbosity,
while my path is strewn with promises casually broken.

Honesty of expression is for the undiplomatic,
never, never, be truly pragmatic;

for to claim an English birthright, your skin must assuredly be
    white.
Was there ever acclaimed an Englishman who to this did not
    conform?

Three months after leaving the air force I had still not been
able to find suitable employment. My gratuity and leave pay
were now exhausted and I was getting desperate. I had already
decided that I might have to return to the air force, but in the
meantime I had to live and provide myself with some spending
money until such time as I made up my mind about a further
period of service. Lyons Corner House in the Strand, who
operated a twenty four hours service was in the habit of
employing servicemen on leave on a casual basis from day to
day. I had myself worked there in the past when on leave and out
of funds. I now applied for a job on a permanent basis and was
offered the post of 'dishwasher' in the kitchen, working from 10
at night until 6 in the morning at £6 per week with meals on
duty. It was not exactly what I was looking for, but beggars can't
be choosers.

I had often wondered what went on behind the scenes in a big
restaurant, as we sit at our comfortable tables lulled by soft
music and watch the immaculately clad waitresses and waiters
dispense tempting fares from gleaming dishes. Haven't we all
tried to picture in our minds eye the goings on in those
mysterious nether regions? Now I would have a chance to find
out. The usual petty jealousies and currying for favour which go
on wherever a large number of people are employed, was very
much in evidence here. There was continual jockeying for
promotion to a higher grade. A restaurant's dishwasher is the
lowest in the order of staffing, and a black dishwasher the
absolute bottom of the barrel.

In this particular restaurant there were six of us to a shift, and,
although there was no official 'chargehand' as such, the senior
employee by virtue of his length of service assumed the role with
the tacit concurrence of the head cook. This individual received
no more pay than the rest of us, the only privilege this position
bestowed on its holder was a chance to lord it over the rest of us,
and the permanent job of washing silver, which was the cleanest
and easiest of the chores. The next in seniority worked at the rear

of the electric dishwasher removing the wire baskets of washed dishes as they moved forward on the conveyor belt. I was of course always delegated to do the dirtiest jobs. Unfair though this was, it did not bother me unduly, I was earning a living of sorts, and doing it honestly. Besides, it was anything but uninteresting.

It gave me an opportunity to study at close hand a class of Englishmen with whom I had had very little contact so far. Some of their personal habits left much to be desired, to say the least, and contrasted ill with the popular, but quite unfounded belief that all black people were hygienically inferior in their habits to whites. For example, there was Bill who made a regular habit of eating tit-bits of customer's left-overs before they were scraped from the plates into the swill bins. Why he should do this was a mystery to me, because we were adequately fed whilst on duty.

Then there was Tommy, whom I named 'the fag roller' because he collected cigarette ends from the ash trays, kept them in a paper bag, and during rest periods methodically broke them up, extracted the tobacco, and re-rolled them into fresh cigarettes. He was himself a moderate smoker, but he made and saved up so many cigarettes from his butt ends, one could not resist the conclusion that he was dealing in second-hand cigarettes among his cronies. It was of course still the days of strict rationing.

Disgusting as these practices were, they did not in any way affect the service which the customers received from our particular department. Unfortunately, the same could not be said for the serving staff by whom the dishes were actually prepared from the waiter's orders. Although there was never any shortage of utensils for handling food, it was nevertheless common practice for junior cooks to use their bare hands to put fish, vegetables and meat on the plates, licking their fingers after each operation. This would be done sometimes even after a visit to the urinals without washing their hands. In fairness to the management it must be stated that there were numerous notices prominently displayed all over the kitchen and toilets, calling the attention of all staff to the need for personal hygiene, and scrupulous cleanliness in the handling of food for the public's consumption. In a large restaurant, however, it is virtually impossible for the management to supervise every individual activity. A lot must of necessity be left to the employee's own sense of decency and cleanliness.

The acute manpower shortage in the immediate postwar years may have forced the catering trade to employ the type of people they would never have considered in normal circumstances. This could have accounted for some of the worst practices, but it could never explain the daily lapses of hygiene by qualified cooks and their assistants. As a result of this experience, it was several years after leaving this employment before I could bring myself to enter a restaurant for a meal, and even today I still do so with a distinct feeling of trepidation. I do not think it would be an exaggeration or unfair comment to say that the standard of food hygiene in England is one of the lowest in Western Europe.

My employment as a dishwasher lasted six months, but in that time I learnt more about the basic character of the English labouring classes than I could have done in years of academic study. Two very firm impressions stand out. Firstly, the British working class display far more unreasonable and blind prejudice against coloured people than do the middle classes, and secondly, that foreign workers are disliked, principally because they tend to show up the indolence and idleness of a sizeable proportion of British workers. On the other hand, the conscientious British worker very rarely resented anyone at work as long as they did their fair share, and expected no special favours. Regrettably, in my experience they were not in the majority.

CHAPTER 6. *Return to the Air Force.*

After six months I had had enough of washing dishes, pots and pans, and since it did not seem I was ever going to obtain suitable employment in the prevailing atmosphere, I was left with no alternative but to return to the Royal Air Force. I therefore signed on for a four years spell of regular service under the 'bounty scheme'. This was an offer to all servicemen below commissioned rank still serving or recently released, to return for a specific number of years not exceeding four, of regular service. On the act of signing, a bounty of £25 would be paid immediately, and for every year of regular service thereafter, a further £25, payable at the end of the engagement. £125 may not seem very much today, but in 1947 that was quite a considerable sum to the average serviceman, enough to give one a start in a small business, or about half the deposit on an average family house.

The question for me now was, what occupation should I follow in the air force for the next four years? This was answered for me by the Air Ministry itself. They were just then advertising for servicemen with a knowledge of legal work for the Army and Air Force Legal Department. Relying on the knowledge gained as a solicitor's clerk in Jamaica, I applied and was accepted after an interview in London. In a couple of months after this I was posted to the Air Ministry Unit, London on their 'special duties list', attached to Eastern Command Legal Aid Division, Hounslow.

On arrival in London to take up my appointment, I discovered that, although I was to live out in civilian quarters, no arrangements had been made for my accommodation. What is more, the Division was not expecting me for another week. So, with absolutely no previous knowledge of this area of London, I had to go out and hunt for digs to move into that very night. My need was so pressing I could ill afford to be choosy or discriminating in my choice. Even so, had I known I was accepting accommodation in a home which housed twenty cats of both sexes and all sizes, I certainly would not have been so eager to accept. Those cats made my life a living hell for the two weeks, which was all I could endure of them.

This boarding house was in Feltham, Middlesex, a short bus journey from Hounslow Heath where I would be actually working. Those cats were everywhere, they occupied every chair in the building, and even my bed. At meal times I had constantly to be removing them from the dining table. It was positively disgusting. At the end of the second week I returned from church on the Sunday to find two of the beastly things sampling my dinner. That was the last straw, I had had enough. Even if it meant walking the streets all night, I could no longer remain under the same roof as those blasted cats. Fortunately such extreme measures were not necessary. I found suitable accommodation that very afternoon through the good offices of the local News Agent who knew all about the cats and was sympathetic. It was with ready cheerfulness that I shook off the dust of my feline abode for more congenial surroundings.

The house, where I found accommodation after the cattery, was one of a neat row of semi-detached in a quiet side street in Hounslow Central. This was an eminently respectable residential area. The house consisted of three bedrooms all on the top floor, a large dining room and kitchen on the ground floor. The only bathroom was also on the top floor, but there was a second toilet on the ground floor. Mr and Mrs Scummer occupied the main bedroom, whilst another bedroom was occupied by their two daughters. The elder of these two was married to an Australian, or it could have been Canadian, and I understood she was then waiting a call to join her husband in his home country where he had returned after serving with the British Forces somewhere in Europe. The call never came while I was still resident in the house. The younger girl was about 15 years old at the time, and a grammer school student.

The other bedroom which overlooked the front garden, and was now occupied by me, belonged to the only son of the family, who was somewhere overseas doing his national service. The decision to take a boarder was only made after his departure abroad. I was therefore their first paying guest. Being new in this field of activity, there was never any of the hard, parsimonious attitude of the professional boarding house keeper. I was always treated as one of the family and become very attached to them.

71

There was one other member of the family whom I have not yet mentioned, the eldest daughter. She was married to a minor civil servant in the Foreign Office, and lived not far away in a nearby village. She was an incurable snob. She felt, perhaps rightly, that she had made a much better marriage than her younger sister, and considered her husband a cut above the rest of the family.

To do him justice, her husband never gave the impression that he shared his wife's views on the subject. In the two years I lived with the family, I can only remember her visiting on three or four occasions at the most, and two of those were at Christmas. Her husband came on numerous occasions, usually on his way home from the office. I had the distinct feeling at the time, that his wife did not know of most of these visits.

It was hard to reconcile the fact that this insufferable snob was the daughter, and sister, of this charming and unassuming family. Papa Scummer, who in his youth was a first class athlete and amateur footballer, took me under his wing, so to speak, right from the very beginning. He never tired of showing off his many trophies consisting of medals and cups of every size which he had won over the years. I learnt more from him about past British athletic achievements than I could have done reading a dozen books written on the subject.

Although well past his 65th year, he was still very active, and did not look a day over 55. One of his main preoccupations was his membership of the British Legion Ex-Servicemen's Club. Through him I soon became a regular visitor to the club. He was an excellent darts player, and was either the present or a past champion of the club, and much respected. Until now, my interest in darts was but a passing one. Under the old man's influence, however, I became a keen and fairly competent player. After I had been visiting the club for about six months, a friendly match was scheduled to take place between the club and a team from a local pub. To my utter amazement I was included in the team to meet the visitors. I had no doubts whatever that Papa Scummer had something to do with it. Whatever the reason for my inclusion, I was expected to meet the standard set by the other members of the team.

It is perhaps difficult for a non-player to fully appreciate how jealous the average darts player is over his club's performance.

To elect a practically unknown novice to compete against a visiting team (even in a friendly game) is unheard of and would be considered sacrilege by most clubs. I was therefore determined to do well, or at least not to let the rest of the team down.

On the night of the big occasion, the match had progressed on a pretty even keel up to the end of the second game. The score was then one game all, with the visitors starting the third and final leg. I was the last thrower of my team. When I came to my last three darts, my opponents were already down to a 'double' to end the game, while we still needed 185. With my first dart I threw a treble twenty, with my second, I took careful aim and threw, again it landed in the treble twenty. There was deathly silence as I shaped up for my third and final throw. It must have been obvious that I was very nervous and I hesitated. Just then Papa Scummer whispered to me, "you can do it, just aim for your last dart, and not the tiny space beside it'. Marshalling all my powers of concentration I aimed for the root of my second dart, and threw. Once the dart left my hand, I closed my eyes dreading to see the result. The next thing I knew I was being lifted shoulder high above the crowd and applauded.

Only then did I look at the dart board, and I could scarcely believe the evidence of my own eyes. All three darts were firmly embedded in the treble twenty, and we had won a game which moments before we seemed certain to lose. It was the custom in those days to concede victory for a throw of three treble 20s, irrespective of the score required.

Everyone was absolutely delighted, even members of the defeated team came over to congratulate me. After this, the drinks flowed freely and fast, so much so that on the way home I was continually stepping over or avoiding non-existent objects in my path. The record of that night's fantastic throw was chalked up above the score board with my name and the date for everyone to see for months to come. On a national scale this performance would probably not be of much significance, but at this level of competition, it was quite an achievement.

Back at the Scummer household I had settled in quite comfortably. Mamma Scummer, a pleasant, well upholstered grandmother of about 55 or 56 was everything a lonely serviceman thousands of miles from home could wish for. She was mother, counsellor, confidante, avenging angel (when the occasion warranted it) and cook par-excellence all rolled into one. Apart from my own parents, I loved and respected her far above anyone else. If I was feeling sad, she would cheer me up with anecdotes of the London blitz. If I was ill she nursed me, and when I got out of line by being late for meals, or left things lying about instead of putting them away, she would scold me in exactly the same manner as any other member of the household. My only problem at that time was her youngest daughter who had a crush on me. In her youthful romantic eyes I was a glamorous war hero who had survived to tell the tale. In her over fertile imagination, she wove a romantic web around me. Once I was admitted to the household she acted as though I was her private property. She scorned the attentions of boys of her own age and thought of them as immature, and imagined herself very sophisticated for so doing.

She made my bed every morning before leaving for school. At the breakfast table, which she laid, there would be a 'love note' under my cereal bowl. Each evening after supper I had to spend half an hour with her over her homework, most of which she was much more competent at doing anyway. In the winter when she turned down my bed each night, she would persist in putting her hot-water bottle in my bed, even when I asked her not to because of my fear of getting chilblains.

The first time I invited a girl friend to the house, she sulked for a week. She would deliberately kick my shins under the table, and every time I reached for sugar, milk, or condiments she managed to get hold of them before I could, and kept me waiting as long as she possibly could, without making her intentions obvious to the others, or so she thought.

The family were fully aware of her crush on me, but treated it with tolerant amusement, to the point of ribbing. The only sensible way to deal with a teenage crush, unless one wanted to invite serious repercussions. She was really a sweet little innocent, and one of the nicest persons it has been my good fortune to have known. If she ever reads this I would like her to know I still have the very fondest memories of my adoptive English kid sister.

I had by now settled in my new job and, in order to better equip myself, I enrolled for three lectures per week at the LCC's

Kennington College of Commerce and Law. My subjects were the law of evidence, contracts and tort. It also had a bearing on my future ambitions as already explained. This course of lectures entailed a lot of travelling between my digs in Hounslow and the college in South London. The need for some form of transportation of my own was keenly felt, so, once again, I bought myself a motorcycle.

Before acquiring the motorcycle my weekend entertainment was generally confined to my immediate surroundings. Now, however, I could and did travel further afield, returning home whenever it suited my convenience, instead of having to make sure I caught the last train or bus. With this greater freedom of mobility I became a regular Saturday night visitor to the Hammersmith Palais de Dance, and that was how I came to meet Marie, an Anglo-Italian girl.

There was only one word to describe Marie, 'gorgeous'. She had jet black hair, just short of shoulder length, dark flashing eyes and very sultry looks, inherited no doubt from her Italian father who had settled in England some years before the war. Her skin was smooth and petal soft, but she had a very determined and tempestuous nature, which only made her the more desirable to me. I saw her for the first time on the dance floor of the Hammersmith Palais on one of my regular Saturday night visits and immediately decided to make a play for her.

With this in mind, I kept her in sight to the end of the dance and positioned myself strategically to ask for the next dance. When it came it was a quickstep, and I was quick off the mark. 'May I have the pleasure of this dance please?' She hesitated briefly, then replied, 'certainly'. She was a very good dancer, and I wasted no time telling her so. She modestly parried the compliment by replying: 'You lead so beautifully, it is easy for me to follow'. Delightfully flattering, and the perfect answer.

I felt sure she was not English and was curious to know her nationality. Choosing my words carefully I said: 'You are too word perfect not to be English, yet, your appearance is distinctly continental'. She reacted exactly as I hoped she would by answering the implied question. 'As a matter of fact I am half English and half Italian, but I was born here in London.' At the end of that dance we sat and talked over a couple of drinks, about her parents and their business, and Jamaica and my family.

We continued dancing together for the remainder of the evening, and when I offered to run her home on the pillion of my motorcycle, she accepted immediately. Before bidding her good night outside her front door, I extracted a promise from her for us to meet again at the following Saturday night's dance. We also exchanged telephone numbers. The urge to steal a goodnight kiss was almost irresistible, but I thought it best not to push too hard, too soon. So far I had every reason to be pleased with my progress. Why risk the chance of spoiling it by being too hasty?

I would just have to contain my impatience until the following Saturday. I had, however, a full itinerary of work lined up for the next four or five days. On Monday and Tuesday I would be attending the law courts in the Strand. Although the Legal Aid Division had no cases in the 'List' for these two days, I would be sitting in as an observer on the hearing of a number of defended divorce cases. My brief was to make notes of any tricky points of law that might arise, such as the 'Admissability of Evidence, or Authorities cited in support of Legal Submissions'. These would be discussed in depth at the Division's weekly discussion session. On the Wednesday I had a witness to interview in Camden Town, and, if it proved to be necessary, I would have to take a statement. Both these assignments were successfully carried out.

On Friday, the eve of my next meeting with Marie, I went to London Airport to see a friend off. On returning at about 2.00 pm I was approaching Firs Drive, Cranbrook, along the then Bath Road on my motorcycle. I was travelling at about 35 to 40 miles per hour, when suddenly a car came out of Firs Drive, turning into the main carriageway without stopping. I immediately applied my brakes, but realised it would be to no avail as I was already practically on top of the car. I steeled myself for the impact, and at the very last moment let go of the handlebars to avoid being dragged along or under the car.

Inevitably I hit the car broadside on, and the last thing I remembered as I catapulted up and over the bonnet, was a tree at the side of the road coming into focus; then darkness. My next semi-conscious recollection was of a number of white-coated forms looking down at me, then more oblivion. When I next awoke to consciousness I was lying in bed at the West Middlesex Hospital, Hounslow.

As soon as the nurse who was keeping watch over me realised I was awake, she bent down and asked me how I felt. 'OK I suppose,' I replied, and tried to sit up only to discover that I could not. Nurse told me to lie still and make no attempt to move as I had had a nasty tumble from my motorcycle and was none too well. Yes, of course, now it was all coming back to me. The turning car, the crash, and the tree. At this point the doctor came, examined me, wrote some notes on my bed-foot chart, told me they would have me up and about in next to no time, and went.

My next visitor was the ward sister, who told me there was a policeman who would like to ask me some questions. 'Do you feel well enough to talk to him? If you do not, just say so.' I nodded my ascent, and she instructed the nurse to show the constable in. When he arrived, she told him, 'we must not overtax his strength at this stage'. He assured her he would be as brief as he possibly could. Turning to me, he asked, 'well, young man, can you give me your name and address?' When these were supplied he realised for the first time that I was a serving airman. I was wearing civilian clothes at the time of the accident as is usual for personnel on the 'special duties list' when off duty.

He then asked for my unit headquarters so that they could be informed of the accident and my present whereabouts, as they might want to transfer me to a military hospital. Irrational as it may seem, my main concern at that moment was for information about my motorcycle. The constable tried to reassure me on that score. 'Don't worry about it, we've got it at the station in safe keeping. As soon as you are well enough to leave hospital you can come and collect it.' At this point sister reappeared and told him his time was up, but that he could come again later in the day after I had had some more rest.

Sure enough, he was back again in the early afternoon full of apologies for disturbing me so soon again, but the loose ends had to be cleared up while the facts were still fresh in my mind. After taking my statement, he supplied me with the name and address of the other driver, also the names and addresses of two eye

77

witnesses who had volunteered statements to the police, putting the blame for the accident squarely on the driver of the car.

As soon as I was able to do so I phoned Marie telling her of the accident. After commiserating with me, she admitted that she thought I had stood her up when I did not return to the Palais as arranged, or phoned to explain why I could not make it. I thought I detected a tone of relief in her voice that she was wrong. She came to visit me the next day with an enormous bunch of flowers, some fruit, and a bottle of tonic wine. From then on she visited every day until I was eventually discharged. By then our romance was developing by leaps and bounds, and by the time I was reasonably able to get about under my own steam, there was a tacit understanding that she was my girl.

The driver of the car involved in the accident was charged by the police with dangerous driving, and at the magistrates court hearing, in which I was a witness, he was found guilty, fined £20, which was a fair sum in those days, and had his licence endorsed. Whilst in hospital I was visited by him on a number of occasions when I informed him that as soon as the police case was out of the way I would be starting a civil action of my own for damages, for personal injuries and compensation for my motorbike, damaged suit and ruined watch. He indicated that he had no intention of disputing my claim except in the amount of damages which would be done by his insurance company in any case. In fact the action was eventually settled out of court to the satisfaction of all concerned.

In addition to my action the Air Ministry sued him for loss of my service during the period of my hospitalization and convalescence. This action I believe was also settled out of court. Due to my long absence from the Legal Aid Section following the accident, on my return to duty there was not an immediate opening for me to fill so I was temporarily posted to the Air Ministry Information Service based in Whitehall. I took up my post at Information 2b, one of many government departments housed at the time in a large rambling edifice overlooking Parliament Square. I believe the information centre has now been merged with another department and moved into more modern accommodation.

The centre was divided into various sections, my particular section was concerned with public relations, and more

78

specifically with the national press. All air force releases to the press originated in this section, even though the original information may have come from elsewhere. My duties could briefly be summarised as:– 'Information relating to change of commands, promotions of high ranking officers, movements of units to and from overseas, and advance release of policy statements by the Minister for Air Force Affairs or his Parliamentary Secretary, to be made from the House of Commons.'

I think I ought to make it clear that not all parliamentary statements were capable of advance release. Another important function of this section was the daily scanning of all national newspapers for articles of criticism of the air force, its officers and ministers. Editorial and comment columns were searched for direct, or oblique references of a disparaging nature. The comments and editorials had to be summarised, and passed to the Minister's parliamentary private secretary with, where appropriate, the relevant facts, figures and documents for refuting the criticisms, or explaining away awkward situations. This work was done seven days per week with a week-end rota of duties to deal with the weekly periodicals and Sunday papers.

The work was extremely interesting and absorbing, especially for someone like myself who had always had a keen interest in the written word. It gave me an opportunity to develop my natural flair in the marshalling of facts and data.

This however is not a narrative on my work at Information 2b, it is only important in so far as it formed a small part of my period on the Air Ministry's Special Duties List. My stay in Whitehall was short lived as I was again needed at Legal Aid Section Hounslow. During this period my relationship with Marie had settled into a steady routine of mutual benefit to us both. One thing however worried me. I was never invited to her home, or met her parents with whom she lived. I naturally thought she was afraid to face the possible disapproval of her parents and neighbours, and the general stigma of having a 'black boyfriend'. Make no mistake about it, at that time any girl who was brave enough to go out with a black man was more than likely to be ostracised by her local community. I started dropping hints about these thoughts of mine as I had every intention of asking her to marry me. Then, and only then, did she tell me that she was already married but separated from her husband. She continued, 'although the marriage is as dead as the proverbial dodo, there was no chance of a divorce as they were both catholics'.

Had the permissive society arrived then, no doubt about it that we would have just lived together, but at the time we were still inhibited by public opinion and the traditional conventions. So we continued our clandestine affair until I left for Jamaica on a legal assignment for Army and Air Force Legal Aid Section Hounslow.

Earlier on in my narrative I mentioned a visit to Camden Town to interview a witness. In fact our client was a Jamaican airman, whose wife was running around at home in Jamaica. After months of fruitless communication with the legal authorities and the commanding officer of the RAF base in Jamaica, it was decided that I should go out to Jamaica and try to wind up the enquiries at that end.

My brief was to make discreet enquiries as to the lady's activities, try to procure sworn statements on affidavits which would establish her adulterous associations and return them to England. At the end of my assignment I was to have a period of home leave before returning to England to rejoin my unit. For the assignment I was provided with a first class return passage by sea and letters of introduction to the commanding officer of RAF Palisadoes and to the Jamaican legal authorities. The commanding officer at Palisadoes, Flight Lieutenant Williams, did not take kindly to the idea of having to provide me, a mere corporal, with the necessary facilities to carry out my assignment. He considered that he had officers of superior rank who were quite capable of undertaking the work assigned to me, forgetting that it was precisely because those officers had failed to deliver, that my presence in Jamaica had become necessary.

In the then context of colonialism it went against the grain for white men in Jamaica to be seen in any other role than that of . the master. Of course there was nothing he could do about it. No way could he ignore or refuse to comply with the Air Ministry's written instructions. Shortly after completing my investigations and therefore when I was on leave, I received a telegram from him asking me to report to Palisadoes at once. I naturally thought he had had some urgent communication for me from London, so I complied. When I arrived at the base, he endeavoured to embarrass me by threatening to charge me with the unauthorised possession of official stationery, which was really ridiculous, as it had been supplied to me by the legal aid section for the specific purpose which he was purporting to challenge.

In fact, on my return to England Flight Lieutenant Williams had no option but to report that I had carried out my assignment with correctness and professional expertise, because I was able to supply my superiors in England with the evidence they required for our client to procure his divorce, which he did about six months after my visit to Jamaica.

On the return voyage to England aboard the 'SS Bayano' four of my fellow passengers were Captain Gammons, conservative Member of Parliament for the constituency of Hornsey, North London, who later became Post Master General in the last Churchill government, and his wife, Mr W. J. Brown, independent labour Member of Parliament for either Rugby or Derby, I am not sure which, and Rabbi Silverman, the senior Jewish Rabbi in Jamaica who was on his way to visit his sister in Manchester, England. During the voyage all four of us men spent most of the journey playing bridge.

When we arrived at Avonmouth, England, there was a seamen's strike in progress. As a result our baggage was not cleared until the following day, and even this was done by clerical staff. I ought to mention here that only the MPs and their two companions, Rabbi Silverman and myself, were so privileged, and a special charabanc was provided to take us to London. We arrived in London late that night and when Captain Gammons discovered that it would not be possible for me to get to my unit that night, he invited me to stay at his Buckingham Palace Mansions flat for the night.

During the voyage from Jamaica I celebrated my 32nd birthday on board ship. The ship's cook baked me a cake, and the guests at my party were Captain and Mrs Gammons, Mr Brown, Rabbi and Mrs Silverman, the ship's master, Captain Jones, the ship's purser, and Flying Officer Redpath who was also returning to England from leave in Jamaica. Mr Brown was writing the final chapter of his book *Jamaican Journey*, and the birthday party was mentioned in the book. I also took part in the ship's concert party singing a couple of calypsos.

An amusing sidelight to this shipboard encounter was the fact that when I finally left the air force and applied for a job with the GPO I had to supply two independent references which was not easy for someone with very limited civilian contacts. By then Captain Gammons was Post Master General in the Conservative government. In desperation I phoned him at his home and sought his permission to use him as one of my references. His wife answered the phone and told me that, although he was out, she was sure I could do so as they have often spoken about me and wondered what had become of me. However, to put my mind at rest she would get him to write and confirm it. Within days I had a letter from his parliamentary private secretary to the effect that the minister remembers our voyage with pleasure, and has no objection to my using him as a reference.

When subsequently the interviewing officer of the GPO saw that one of my references was no other than the PMG himself, he refused to accept that it could be genuine. My reply was, 'if you cannot take my word, then ring the House of Commons (and I gave him the number) and verify it', which he did.

Needless to say I not only got the job, but the word went around that everyone should be extremely careful of their dealings with me as I was a friend of the PMG. Unfortunately, this did not help me very much because I was viewed as a possible management spy, which was ironic, because I was, if anything, a rebel against some very archaic conditions and practices which existed in the telephone service at that time.

CHAPTER 7. *Tour of France 1951*

Before a second attempt to breach the employment barrier I decided I would treat myself to a continental holiday and renew a war-time friendship with a French colleague. In the company of my English friend, Bob, I set out to tour France on my motorcycle. In order to minimise on hotel bills we provided ourselves with a couple of small bivouac tents and booked passages on the cross-channel ferry through the RAC, who provided us with route maps, hotel lists and arrangements for breakdown repairs on the continent. Early one Friday morning in early May we set out from London for the channel port of Dover. We arrived in Dover at 7.00 am, boarded the cross-channel steamer 'Dinnard', and sailed at 8.30 am for Boulogne. The crossing was quiet and uneventful. At Boulogne dis-embarkation was surprisingly quick and efficient. The RAC had prepared our travelling 'Carnets' and all we had to do was report to their agent who met the ferry. In a little over half an hour we were directed to our motorcycles at the quayside, given final instructions, re road conditions and repair facilities and reminded to travel on the right of the road. In spite of this final reminder, when we left Boulogne for Paris we immediately drove off on the left of the road from force of habit, until a crowd of furiously gesticulating Frenchmen drew our attention to the fact. Habit dies hard, but it was to be our only lapse of this nature for the remainder of the holiday.

From Boulogne we took the main arterial road through Montreuil, Abbeyville, Beauvais, Pontoise and St Denis; entering Paris through the Ponte de la Chapelle. Travelling was very rough as the roads were bumpy and pitted with shell holes from the war. Very little had so far been done to repair the ravages of the war. To add to our discomfort it started to rain quite heavily just before Beauvais, and except for short spells, continued to do so until we were within a couple of miles of the outskirts of Paris. On arrival in the capital we felt rather silly being completely soaked and mud-bespattered while the city basked in brilliant sunshine.

We made our way to the centre of the city, crossed the Place de la Concorde bridge, through the Porte de Champeret to the Avenue de Verdun in Courbevoie, where my war-time friend and his family lived. On arrival we were given a warm welcome by Madame and Monsieur Gouffe and their daughter Simione. Joseph, my friend and the only son of the family, was still at work, but expected home any minute. The Gouffe's English was very sketchy to say the least, and our French ran only to a few set phrases. Consequently our attempts at polite conversation whilst we awaited the arrival of Joseph developed into a veritable pantomime of half-English, half-French, and a thousand gesticulations. We were however able to convey our desire for a bath, and managed this by the time Joseph arrived home.

We retired early that first night as we were very tired from our long and arduous travel. In the afternoon of the next day, which was Saturday, we decided to try the Paris metro on our own. Our first surprise was to discover that we could not book from point 'A' to point 'B' as we would on the London underground. Instead we had to purchase a book of tickets and when getting off the station tender the appropriate ticket for that particular journey. Our inexperience of the system and lack of French caused considerable merriment among the other travellers and metro employees. One place, or rather facility, caused us considerable embarrassment and trepidation, the French 'public convenience'. Both women and men used the same entrance contrary to all our previous experience. Once inside the correct cubicle the biggest surprise of all was encountered. There was no accommodation for sitting down as was customary here in England, instead there were just a couple of metal 'footprints' over which you stooped. It had to be seen to be believed.

Oh to be in Paris in the spring; there was so much we wanted to see and so little time in which to do it. We could only manage 48 hours for the capital as we intended travelling to Nice and Monte Carlo on the Riviera. Where better to start our sightseeing than the top of the Eiffel Tower? And what a view it was from that vantage point. Paris lay below us like a gigantic star with the Arc de Triomphe and Place de la Concorde forming the centre from which the various avenues and boulevards radiate to form the points of the star.

From the Eiffel Tower we went to the Arc de Triomphe and had our photographs taken by Simione, standing by the tomb of the 'Unknown Warrior' with its perpetually burning flame. That was followed by a visit to Notre Dame Cathedral, and a quick climb of its winding stairs which reminded me of climbing up St Pauls in London. At the top more photographs were taken with the River Seine in the background, and the cathedral gardens in the foreground. From Notre Dame our next stop was the offices of Air France where Simione worked. This was followed by a meal at a restaurant near the Lafayette Galleries.

In the evening Simione and Joseph took us to a night club in Montparnasse to get some atmosphere, as they put it. It soon became clear, however, that this was as much an innovation for them as it was for us, as they were completely ignorant of the club's routine and asked as many questions as we did ourselves. This club had the luxury of two bands, one white and one negro. The negro band played Latin American dance music while the white played orthodox European dance music. Both bands were of fairly good standard, but the 'floor show' at midnight was second rate, and to be honest rather mediocre. I am afraid our introduction to Paris 'night life' was a disappointment after the hair-raising anecdotes we had had from returning British servicemen.

Practically all the next day was spent in the Montmartre district. This was a cross between Chelsea and Soho in London. Here were assembled the art studios, pavement cafes and strip clubs. Tourists could buy anything from rude post cards to sex. This was of course before the puritanical clean-up of the De Gaulle era. The pavement cafes, with their striped sun shades over tables and bearded artists displaying their paintings, mostly of nude or semi-nude women, gave the place a kind of pseudo Bohemian atmosphere. No visit to Montmartre would be complete without a call at the Sacre Coeur cathedral, or a ride on the vertical railway which runs almost from its steps to Montparnasse below, so, naturally we did both.

We had taken in as much as it was possible to do in the limited time at our disposal, and retired at a reasonable hour to bed as we had to be up at the crack of dawn next morning to check our bikes and pack our gear for an early start on the next leg of our journey. In the morning Madame Gouffe made us sandwiches of crusty French bread filled with strips of smoked ham for the day's journey. Joseph gave us a flask of cognac and a bag of lump sugar with verbal instructions for their use when fatigued by long driving. The method was to saturate one or two lumps of the sugar with cognac and suck slowly. This had the effect of reviving our flagging energies and I was destined to reap the benefit of his thoughtfulness long before the tour was over.

The Gouffes were great connoisseurs of wine and no wonder as one branch of the family owned quite extensive vineyards in the Yonne valley. In my one weekend with the family I learnt more about wines than I had done all my life before. At 9.30 on the Monday morning we bade farewell to our hosts with a promise to keep them informed of our progress to the South of France. Joigny was to be our first overnight stop on the long run to Nice and Monte Carlo. We departed Paris by way of the Porte d'Italie making for the forest of Fontainebleau with a detour to Barbizon; once the home of Rousseau, Millet and Stevenson, and known as the 'Artists's Village'.

Our first main objective was, of course, the fabulous Royal Palace and Forest of Fontainebleau. The palace, which consists of a number of very lovely buildings and elegant apartments, was at the time the headquarters of the British Commander of the Allied Land Forces in Europe. Because of this we were unable to enter any of the buildings or apartments, and this was a bitter disappointment to us. However, by producing my Air Force identity card, we were given permission to enter the gardens for a short look around. After inspecting the gardens we lingered in the forest for several hours admiring the many varied and majestic trees of many nationalities that grew there, and had our sandwiches washed down with red wine in this beautiful setting before continuing our journey southwards.

From Fontainebleau we travelled to Pont-Sur-Yonne and Sens. The latter, a very ancient archbishopric with a see's palace. We arrived in Joigny, a wine growing area on the River Yonne, with just enough daylight left for a short visit to the church of St Thibault, built in the 16th century; and the

Chateau Neuf, built in 1550 but which was now a school. We then found accommodation for the night at a large 'Routier' just off the main highway of the town. Routiers in France are the equivalent of transport cafes in England, but better appointed. They were much cheaper than normal hotels, offering a good night's rest, fair meals and a goodish selection of wines at very reasonable prices.

Again we had an early night for a prompt start next morning as we hoped to make Lyon that day, a distance of about 180 to 200 miles. This route took us to Avallon, passing through Auxerre and Vermenton with wooded valleys on either side of the road. Auxerre is the chief town of the Yonne Department, and was badly damaged during the war. It is also very well known for its Chablis wine. From Avallon we enjoyed a view of some of the most picturesque and undulating scenery leading to the vineyards of Burgundy and on to Chalon s. Saône. At Chalon we stopped for a couple of hours to take in a visit to the hospital with its superb panelling and stain glass windows, and a quick look at the Denoun Museum. This was another of the towns with visible signs of war damage. From Chalon to Mâcon along the valley of the River Saône, the road was particularly good and we were able to make excellent time.

We were now getting used to a curious phenomenon; whenever we were approached or overtaken by a British registered vehicle, the occupants would wave furiously and hoot on their horns. There was no mistaking the British origin of the vehicles because of the 'GB' plates prominently displayed at front and rear. We were ourselves supplied with similar plates by the RAC. Before long we were also indulging in this nostalgic display of solidarity. Between Chalon and Lyon we were travelling through farmlands and wine-growing country.

Some of the vineyards which borderd the route added a peculiar beauty of their own to the general scenery. For long stretches of road the scene was of vast fields of beautiful shiney grapes which made our mouths water in anticipation. And so to Lyon, perhaps one of the oldest cities in France. It was founded in 41 BC by the Celts of Gaul. The Emperor Nero and Trajan are said to have built many fine temples there. It has a lovely cathedral and zoological and botanical gardens. My most vivid memory of it is of cobblestones, tramcars and hordes of pedal cyclists. In this, if in no other way, it reminded me of Manchester, England.

We did not stop in Lyon, but continued on the road towards Vienne, which is very flat, and therefore provided excellent ground for camping out. A few miles short of Symphorien d'Ozon we made camp on farmland close to the banks of the River Rhône about half a mile off the main road. We pitched our small tents about 300 yards to the right of a small bridge over the river. In the morning we went down to the water's edge via some stone steps below the bridge to do our washing. This completed, we noticed for the first time a farm house some little distance from the river, and decided to go over and see if we could purchase a jug of milk or some home-made bread and cheese. There was a five-barred gate about 100 yards out from the building and as we could see no one about, we called out. A dog began barking at the sound of our voices and came bounding towards us. Bob was rather scared and was all for leaving at once. Being a dog lover myself I saw no reason for making such an inglorious retreat, and held my ground.

Before the dog could get to the gate a sharp command in French rang out, the dog stopped in its tracks almost immediately, but continued barking. The owner of the voice then appeared from one side of the house. Its possessor was a tall greying man with very bushy eyebrows and a pleasant face. I would say he was about 45 or 46 years old and greeted us in a booming voice, 'Bonjour Messieurs'. 'Bonjour Monsieur,' we replied. 'Por possible obtaine lait?' I hoped this would be interpreted as a request for milk. Smiling broadly, no doubt at the mutilation of his native tongue, he replied, 'Oui Monsieur.' 'Combien (how much)?' I asked. 'Gratis, gratis Monsieur.' Here I decided to venture into the unknown with barely remembered school boy French. 'C'est tres gentil a vous.' This was followed by a veritable torrent of French which I could neither follow or understand. Sheepishly I replied, 'no comprende'. Whereupon the farmer took hold of my hand indicating that we were being invited to follow him to the house. Inside the house he presented his wife who was already waiting our arrival in the front hall. She was very pretty, even in her sober farm clothes and I guessed about 35 years old. She invited, or rather indicated that we should be seated.

88

At this stage a rapid interchange of conversation took place between wife and husband, whereupon she bowed herself out of the room, only to return a very few minutes later with a small table which she proceeded to lay for two, explaining that they had already eaten. We were given coffee with milk, home-made bread, and two boiled eggs each. After this welcome repast we were shown around the farmyard. There were Rhode Island Reds and Leghorn chickens, goats and pigs, a small wooden press, which we gathered without being told, was used for crushing grapes for their home made wine. Before our departure our hosts gave us a large paper bag containing apples, grapes, a few hard-boiled eggs, a bottle of home-made wine. Both walked with us to the gate and remained there waving to us until we were out of sight.

We travelled all that day making only two brief stops, one for lunch and the other to replenish our stock of cold meat, bread and soft drinks. Avignon was reached about two in the afternoon. That night and part of the following day we spent there seeing the sights. The places we particularly wanted to see were the famous 'Broken Bridges', the Pope's Palace, built in 1335, the cathedral of Notre Dame, and the beautiful gothic church, which is over 700 years old. It was here in Avignon that we met Major Dennis and his charming Egyptian wife Fatima. We were having difficulty explaining to the receptionist at the routier that we required a bath before dinner, when the Major who was waiting to make a similar request offered his services as interpreter.

At dinner we sat at the same table and formally introduced ourselves. The Major and his wife were on their way to Nice for a fortnight's holiday where they had rented a flat just off the Promenade des Anglais. When told that we had not made any arrangements for our accommodation, they invited us to share the flat. Fatima explained that the flat was really too large for two people, but that they found from past experience this was the most economical way to spend a holiday in the resort. They would do their own shopping and cooking, and the concierge did the cleaning and changed the linen. I thought it would be great fun shopping and helping with the cooking. I have always rather fancied myself as a cook and love to prepare rather exotic salads, but the biggest bonus of all for us was that our language difficulties would be solved for the time being. Both Fatima and Dennis spoke fluent French. The only disadvantage was the fact that having travelled this route many times before, they were disinclined to make as many sightseeing stops on the way as we would have liked, but this was a small price to pay for having our accommodation and language problems solved for us in one fell swoop.

We did, however, manage a stop at Aix-en-Provence long enough to take some pictures of the beautiful cascading fountain. At Dennis's suggestion we also made a brief stop at the old walled Roman town of Frejus. This is the alleged birth place of Agricola, the Roman general, and was once ravaged by the Saracans. It nestles at the foot of an almost vertical run down from Maximin. Some years subsequent to our visit it was the scene of a most awful disaster when the dam above the town burst, flooding the valley. The loss of life and property was frightening. Whilst there, we noticed that a bullfight was advertised for the following Sunday afternoon, and decided we would travel the 40 or so kilometres back from Nice to attend it. From Frejus we took the route which brought us to the quaint little village of St Raphael, then on to Agay, Le Trayas, Miramar and Cannes. This is the coastal route, a bit longer than the one over the Esteral mountains, but much more picturesque. Cannes, as everyone knows, is perhaps the most popular of the French Riviera resorts with some of the most beautiful and expensive hotels anywhere in France. The run from Cannes to Nice is only 25 kilometres, but full of pure optical coastal delights. It passes through many famous holiday resorts, principal among them being, Juan-Les-Pins and Antibes.

We arrived at Nice in the late afternoon of Thursday and went straight to the flat which was in the Rue Massena, just behind and parallel to the Promenade des Anglais. It consisted of two medium-sized bedrooms, a large lounge, and kitchen with built-in cupboards on the first floor. The furniture was rather dated but comfortable. On Friday morning Fatima and I went to the market which is in the new town to purchase provisions for the week-end whilst Dennis and Bob went swimming. Fatima advised me to leave the bargaining to her during our shopping expedition. It was not long before I appreciated the wisdom of her decision. Her performance with the local trades people was impressive to say the least. Her ability to beat down prices after lengthy bartering saved us at least the cost of a day's rations.

Bearing in mind the fact that the permissive society had not yet reached England, I never stopped marvelling at how little clothes were worn by the average tourist, particularly the women. They seemed to be constantly vying with each other to see who could shed the greatest quantity of clothing at any given time. Some of the bathing outfits would have done justice to the most uninhibited strip-tease artist. The following day which was Saturday, Dennis drove us all to Monte Carlo by way of the 'Grande Corniche' with its majestic mountain and marine scenery. The road winds upwards like some giant snaking labyrinth to emerge at Monte Carlo, the summit. Monte, of course, is the capital of the tiny principality of Monaco. The commercial quarter near the harbour La Condomine is extremely quaint and beautiful. Also of interest and beauty are the Cathedral Gardens, and Oceanic Museum. The centre of attraction, however, is the famous casino built on the top of the cliffs immediately overlooking the Mediterranean.

We did not enter the casino on this occasion as we would be returning on Sunday night to play the 'tables'. The object of today's visit was to explore the principality, savouring its scenic beauties and buying souvenirs. The return journey to Nice in the late afternoon was by way of the lower, or 'Petite Corniche' through Cap-D'ail, Eze-sur-Mer, Beaulieu and Ville Franche. Immediately after lunch on Sunday, which Fatima prepared, we departed for Frejus and the bullfight. We arrived at the Place de Toros to find a huge crowd already assembled and a band playing martial music. We procured seats in the centre stands and settled down to await proceedings. The main attraction on this occasion was to be a visiting matador, 'El Negro' from Spain. The proceedings began with an impressive and colourful parade of matadors in fancy costumes.

Their capes, which were slung over one shoulder, were held in front with one hand while the other was swung backwards and forwards in the manner of marching soldiers. The parade, which lasted about 15 or 20 minutes, was followed almost immediately by the announcement of the first fight. The matador entered the ring with his cape slung over his shoulder, made a bow to the spectators with a sweeping flourish of his hat, then turned to face the gate from which the bull would appear any moment. The first bull was a moderately large one. It charged into the ring rather aimlessly as if trying to get its bearings. Suddenly it caught sight of the matador, lowered its head, pawed the ground, and rushed towards him. The matador, who was standing perfectly still and erect with his cape held in front of his body, started to shake the cape and stamp his feet as though inviting the animal to come and get it.

The implied challenge was accepted by the bull which rushed forward towards the challenger. At what seemed the last possible moment before the bull reached him, he made the slightest of body swerves, and with a deft sweep of the cape avoided the bull's charge.

Pivoting slowly and gracefully he again faced the bull; the stamping of the feet and shaking of the cape was again repeated, while at the same time saying 'Toro, Toro', inviting the bull to have another go. Again the bull charged, and once again he brought into use his gentle and artistic play of the cape. These passes were repeated with subtle variations over and over again until the bull apparently exhausted in its vain attempts to gore its tormentor, stood still with its head lowered as if admitting defeat. At this stage the matador was handed a fresh cape and sword and straight away advanced on the bull with the sword concealed behind the cape but held in front of his body. The cape was held low towards the ground in front of the bull. While the bull's attention was momentarily taken up in contemplation of the cape the matador withdrew the sword from behind the cape and plunged it into the neck of the beast. Other swords were produced and each in turn plunged into the animal's neck until the swords, or 'Bandorillos' as I believe they are called, were sticking out all over the bull's neck like so many unconnected horns.

Finally he was handed a long and shiny sword with which the 'coup de grace' was administered. The poor creature, doubtless in great pain, rushed about bewildered before mercifully collapsing dead. The matador received a great ovation from the spectators, the most vociferous among them being the women. The crowning distaste for me was when the ring master severed the bull's ears and presented them to the matador as a token of his prowess. There is no denying the grace and artistry of the matador. but I felt an almost uncontrollable wave of sympathy for the bull and abhorrence at the blatant cruelty of this national sport. I had had enough of this brutal spectacle and asked to be excused from the party for the remainder of the performance. I spent the next couple of hours wandering around the ancient walls of the town before returning to a small cafe near the bull ring as previously agreed.

On the drive back to Nice I was continually being chided for my squeamishness, and by no one more so than Fatima who seemed to have enjoyed every moment of the gruesome slaughter. Back in Nice we had a quick wash and change, and were off again within a couple of hours for the casino at Monte Carlo. Bob and I were not gaming enthusiasts but felt we had to have a session at the tables to complete our experience. Dennis was obviously an old hand at the tables and was prepared to gamble far in excess of what we wished or could afford, but being the gentleman he was, he suggested we limited our outlay to 10,000 francs each, a total of 30,000 francs (£30 at the then rate of exchange). For the first hour Bob and I had beginner's luck and were winning about 45,000 francs between us. Dennis, on the other hand, had barely managed to remain afloat on his 10,000 francs. Fatima who was not playing had decided on a ruse to get us men away from the tables the moment it became obvious that our luck had turned.

Suddenly the dice started running against Bob and I, and we were rapidly losing our erstwhile winnings. Fatima suddenly pretended she was having one of her 'migraine' attacks, and asked to be taken home. At a check up of funds in the car we were just over 16,000 francs to the good between us, quite a satisfactory result altogether. We had had the excitement and experience of the 'tables' and had made a profit to boot. On Monday Bob and I left to visit Menton near the Italian border, while Fatima and Dennis went on to Antibes. We had enjoyed the scenery of the Grande Corniche so much on our first visit to Monte that we decided to use this route again for the journey to Menton. We were going along quite nicely some distance from Nice, just short of Eze, when suddenly round a bend we were faced with two cars overtaking.

As all motorists know this is a most dangerous practice at the best of times, but absolutely suicidal on a road as narrow and winding as this one was. I was forced off the road and into the ditch. Fortunately for me, we were travelling up hill and not down, or I would surely have gone over the cliff edge with a drop of several hundred feet. Bob miraculously had a clear passage. As it was, I sustained a puncture, a dented front wheel and a broken spring. By some chance I did not come off the bike, but by the time I had righted it and come to a stop the two cars had already disappeared. I was very badly shaken, and even without the damage to the bike, the trip to Menton would have to be called off for that day at least.

I was pushing the bike towards Nice, taking turns with Bob for about five kilometres, when a lorry came along and offered me a lift which I gladly accepted whilst Bob followed on his bike. Once in Nice I immediately sought out the garage on my RAC list for the necessary repairs. The garage people were very sympathetic and cooperative; they would repair the puncture and the damaged front wheel at once, but the replacement spring would have to be ordered from Paris as they did not have one of the correct size in stock. A phone call was made to the suppliers in Paris who promised to put one on the first available train. With any luck it should reach us by Tuesday afternoon. If this forecast proved correct the bike would be ready for collection by lunch-time on Wednesday at the latest.

Our deadline for leaving the resort was Thursday morning, so in spite of the accident I could relax and enjoy the remainder of the holiday. When I called the garage on Wednesday I was told the spring had not arrived on the Tuesday afternoon or Wednesday morning trains. The next train was not due until late that evening, so there was no point calling again until about mid-morning on Thursday. At 11 am on the following day I again called at the garage; still the spring had not arrived. Another phone call was made to Paris to confirm that the spring had indeed been despatched. Confirmation was received, but due to a strike by transport workers in Paris it was only that very morning that they were able to get the spring to the station for despatch. In fact it did not reach Nice until 7 o'clock that evening.

On written instructions from the garage I collected it from the station myself that night and took it into the garage first thing Friday morning. Although the work was completed in just over an hour, by the time I got back to the flat and packed my gear it was midday before I left on the long return journey to Paris (700 miles) and then to Boulogne, my port of embarkation. The ferry back to England was due to sail at 2.30 pm on Saturday. This meant I would have to travel nearly 800 miles in just 26 hours. The original plan was for us to leave on Thursday travelling by way of the Maritime Alps up to Grenoble, and rejoining our inward route at Chalon.

This plan now had to be scrapped. Instead Bob left on Thursday using the same route we used on the inward journey, making his way straight for the Gouffes to alert them of my late arrival. I would follow as soon as I could. I left Nice just after midday and made my first stop at Aix-en-Provence for lunch in the late afternoon and was soon on my way again. From Aix I travelled non-stop to Maçon which I reached about 10 at night. Between Maçon and Tournus I stopped and rested by the side of the road for an hour and a quarter. This had become necessary from sheer fatigue.

Already I had to resort to my cognac and sugar stimulant several times. It worked like a charm for the first couple of occasions, but after that the effect was less evident, and I was finding it increasingly difficult to focus the road ahead, particularly when approached by other vehicles using their headlights. I lost valuable time by this stop but it was preferable to arrive late, than not to arrive at all. The remainder of the drive from Tournus to Paris was a nightmare. For this part of the journey I was resorting to the cognac and sugar every hour, with less and less effect each time. On one occasion I actually dozed off, and was awakened only just in time to avoid running off the road. This near mishap jerked me back to wakefulness for the remainder of the journey.

I finally reached Paris just after six in the morning and made for the Gouffes residence. It is just as well that Bob had insisted in going on ahead to explain the situation. They were already up when I arrived, and had a hot drink ready for me. I followed this with a quick bath, and retired to bed to snatch a few precious hours sleep before setting out on the ride to Boulogne. Bob woke me at 10.30 with ample time for a meal before leaving at 11.30. We arrived at Boulogne after an uneventful trip just before 2 pm expecting to go aboard immediately, only to discover that the ferry would be arriving two hours late owing to bad weather conditions in the channel. Instead of sailing at 2.30, we would now be sailing at 6.00 pm, a whole three-and-a-half hours more which I could have spent in bed. That was the biggest rub of all.

CHAPTER 8. *Back to Civvy Street.*

At the end of my five years regular service I took my discharge, and again directed my efforts to the task of breaking the colour barrier in the jobs market. If you are asking yourself why five years when I had signed on for four? The answer is that the Korean War had started before my four years expired, and under King's Rules and Air Council Instructions, I was obliged to do an extra year's service since a national emergency was once again in operation.

My attempt to breach the civilian employment barrier this time met with better success than did my immediate postwar efforts. I landed my first job as a GPO night telephonist, and after six weeks of intensive theory at London Wall and 'dummy operating' at Kensington, followed by another three weeks of practical work under supervision, I was sent to the long distance and toll exchanges based in Faraday Building, near St Pauls Cathedral in the city.

Here it may be useful to telephone users in general if I give a brief description of what actually used to go on in the average telephone exchange. For instance, if a number of signals, which represented numbers dialled, appeared at about the same time on an operator's area of panel, he or she had no way of knowing which was first dialled. He simply plugged into the nearest one which might very well be the last one that had been dialled. So, if you had to wait for the operator to answer your call, you could imagine he was deliberately ignoring you whilst he indulged in a cup of tea, which seemed to be the popular view.

The only calls which were given immediate and top priority attention were emergency calls for police, fire brigade, and ambulance services. There are of course others such as coast guards and flood warning services, but these were not as well known to the general public as the first three named. The reason the emergency service got such immediate attention was because the 999 position in each exchange was specially located, and always manned by a senior operator. In addition to this, as soon as the three digits were dialled, a big prominent red light glowed over the position, and a hooter which could be heard all over the exchange set up a hell of a din until the signal was answered. Another aspect of the emergency service, which was sometimes not fully understood by the public, was the fact that when someone dialled 999 they were not automatically connected to the police, fire, or ambulance as the case might be. The signal was always answered in the first place by a telephone operator in the exchange of the district from which the call was made.

The operator then had to ascertain from the caller the service required, i.e. police, fire or ambulance. One other bit of information was of vital importance: 'the number of the telephone from which the call was being made'. This was necessary because so often a caller in her or his agitation of the moment forgot to give the police or fire brigade the address at which the service was needed. Whenever this happened the operator could then pin-point, or at worse narrow down, the area from which the call came, and so save valuable time which might very well mean the difference between life and death or severe damage to property.

The telephone service operated a 24 hour service to the public split into roughly two through-night duties and four short duties. It was the duty of the exchange supervisor or senior telephonist in-charge to check lines to emergency authorities at least once per day to see that they were in good working order. In addition some of the emergency services did their own checking by dialling the exchange at varying times of the day and night.

When these checks were made, the two operators involved had to exchange names, which were entered on a record of testing with the time and date of the checks. One of the first duties of a relieving supervisor was to inspect this record to see that the scheduled tests had been carried out by the outgoing staff. By these elaborate checks and counter checks the GPO ensured that whenever an emergency service was required the call would go through immediately without any delay due to technical faults.

During the two years I spent at trunks a common practice among male telephonists, when they wanted to keep social engagements which could not be fitted in with their tour of duty, was to canvas their associates who had the appropriate night off duty and try to make a swap. If the operator was unwilling to make a straight swap, then he would be asked to 'substitute' at a price over and above what he would normally receive from the GPO for that night's duty. Some operators made such a good thing of this practice, that the department was forced to lay down maximum hours of duty which any operator could do without a clear 24 hours rest between spells of duty.

At trunks there was very little sentiment or esprit de corps among the night staff, it was every man for himself and the devil take the hindmost. These practices may not apply at the moment, but they certainly did in the 1950's. It is conceivable that with the amount of automation today, coupled with the improved pay of telephonists, the necessity for these practices may no longer exist.

I found the life of a telephonist anything but dull; all sorts of queer situations arose from time to time. There was the old lady living alone, who woke up in the middle of the night to discover that her tom cat was out on the tiles for the night, and then rang her local exchange with the request that someone be sent immediately to look for her Moggy, as she was terrified that he may be taking up with one of the alley cats of the area. Of course she was prepared to pay compensation to the operator for his troubles to the tune of ten shillings (50p) and a glass of sherry when he got to the house (it was winter and very cold), which for an old age pensioner in those days was a princely sum. It took the best part of half an hour to convince her that her request and offer could not be met or accepted.

Then there was the widow nearing middle age who invited me to tea because my voice sounded so much like that of her doctor's, and she was intrigued to meet the man behind the voice. When told that it was most unlikely that I would be anything like her doctor as I was a coloured colonial, she was still not deterred. If anything her curiosity became greater. After some little time the invitation was accepted. I will say no more than that she lived somewhere in Essex, and I had to catch a train from Liverpool Street to a station a few miles from her home.

She met me at the station in her prewar vintage car which

99

was still in very good condition. She was a slim dark haired woman of about 43 or 44 years old although she only admitted to 40. The house was a two storey affair set in its own grounds about a quarter of a mile from its nearest neighbour.

There were apple trees in the back garden and a beautiful flower border in the front with a small well-kept lawn. I was introduced to a daughter of 17 and a son of 15 years old. Her husband had died a few years earlier leaving her reasonably comfortable. Apparently he had been something in the city, owned the house outright, some shares and a good insurance cover for his family provided the value of money did not fall too drastically over the years.

Mrs, I will call her, Smith (although that was not her name) was no beauty, but she had very good dress sense and used her make-up with a professional touch. She had an almost uncanny ability to do just the right thing to emphasize her good points and play down the unflattering ones. When thus turned out, she made a very attractive and desirable figure that would appeal to most men. What surprised and mystified me was why she felt the need to have to resort to the ruse she used with me? And even more baffling, when she met me, was what on earth did she see in me? Maybe she thought it would be safe to have a secret affair with me without compromising herself in her local community, but that's just surmise on my part because I just could not come up with a logical explanation.

On my first visit to tea I was persuaded, without much effort, to spend the night. It was therefore no great surprise, when just before 2 am Beatrice (again not her real name) joined me in bed in the guest room. I will spare the reader the hoary details of that visit, except to say, 'she was hungry, and a damned good eater'. Next morning at breakfast I had an uncomfortable feeling that the daughter knew of our early morning assignation. Not that she said or did anything in particular to suggest that she knew, but on a number of occasions I caught her making overt glances from her mother to myself, in which to my guilty conscience she was saying, 'you think I don't know, but I do'.

On the other hand it could have been sheer curiosity because of my colour. Be that as it may, I felt so uncomfortable, it was with relief that I took my departure of the children shortly after breakfast and was driven back to the station by Beatrice. In my

100

subsequent visits over a period of about nine months, I developed a really close association with the children, who were much nearer to my own age group than they were to their mother's. The association ended, as I said, after about nine months, not because of any disagreement or waning of ardour, but because I met and fell in love with a Jamaican student nurse, and almost at the same time I had the transfer I had been hoping for to the Riverside Exchange at Hammersmith. This enabled me to quietly drop out of the life of the Smith family without having to make tedious excuses. Although I felt very bad at taking such a cowardly way out, I was able to convince myself that it was the best course for all concerned.

Having written so much about my extra marital relationships, it is only fair that I should expand a little about my marriage. It was love at first sight for me when I met my wife Ivy May Pottinger at the wedding reception of the niece of an old family friend. I wooed and married her within the year, but before very long I realised I had made a terrible mistake. When a marriage breaks down it's very rarely that only one party is at fault; mine was no exception. We were temperamentally unsuited to each other. Both of us were very strong characters who did not find it easy to accommodate each other's ambitions, or make allowance for the strains that being black in a white orientated society put on us. Inevitably the marriage broke down, but not before she had borne me two lovely daughters of whom I am very proud.

Both my daughters have gained honours degrees from university, and the entire credit for their educational success must go to their mother for making an excellent job of bringing them up without a husband at her side for most of their young lives. After the divorce, which I instituted, there was a traumatic period when I lost touch with the children for a number of years. I am however happy to record that after some difficult readjustments I have been able to re-establish and maintain a very good working relationship with my daughters again. Even my ex-wife and I are able to meet and enjoy the company of our children and grandson without rancour.

I remained a telephone operator for just over six years, by which time I felt sufficiently confident to offer my resignation to the GPO in order to seek a career in a more competitive and financially rewarding field. In this respect I was fortunate enough to obtain employment in the textile, and later fashion, or 'rag trade' as it is popularly called. My first job was as a warehouse clerk with Khan's Textiles of Upper Regent Street, at their Harrow Road depot.

Within a matter of weeks a vacancy occurred at the Regent Street building due to the serious illness of the stock room supervisor, and I was recommended by the Harrow Road depot manager for the post on a strictly temporary basis. Before leaving his words to me were, 'Eddie your talents are being wasted here, you are obviously capable of better things, here is your opportunity to show them at head office that it would be a waste of talent to send you back here'. I certainly had no intention of returning to Harrow Road, and did not intend to waste this opportunity to impress the powers that be. I therefore set out to show my ability and general efficiency, and it paid off. I was confirmed in the post, and when my predecessor returned from sick leave, he was offered another position in the firm which he accepted.

After two years at Khan's I felt it was time for me to move on and up. I then secured a position with Shubette of Great Portland Street as head of their complaints department. This job suited me ideally as my main function was to deal with customers complaints from our retail outlets, pouring oil on troubled waters so to speak. In practice, getting our stockists off the hook without laying my employers open to legal action or adverse publicity for their products.

Whilst employed at Shubette, three former Jamaican airmen and myself founded one of the first West Indian political pressure groups in this country after the war, The West Indian National Association, and produced our own national magazine called *WINA*. I was physically involved in the production of the magazine, writing the monthly fashion page under the nom de plume of 'Miss WINA Couture', I also wrote regular political articles putting our point of view on issues of the day. Unfortunately both the Association and the magazine folded up after about three years. The former through internal power struggles and apathy of the rank and file members, and the magazine because of our inability to attract advertising revenue. Before this came about, however, we had one memorable lease

102

of life when we were able to organise a reception and dance in honour of the visiting West Indian cricket team under the captaincy of Frank, later Sir Frank, Worrell at Porchester Hall, Bayswater. It was such a financial success, we were able to wipe out an operating deficit of over £300, and continue to publish for another six months.

Our attempt to organise our countrymen into a cohesive political force for mutual protection met with failure, but my own personal career was now well established at long last. Nothing spectacular if one was white, but being who I am in the prevailing atmosphere of the time, I had justifiable reasons to feel I was making the big break through. I had by now built up a reputation in the fashion trade as a competent, conscientious and hard working operator. As a result I was able to move from one 'House' to another among the leading West End fashion houses, gaining more and more experience, and always at an enhanced salary, until I eventually landed the job of stock control supervisor with a firm trading under the name of Gay Girl at their main production centre in the East End of London, with show rooms just off Oxford Circus.

Apart from the relatively high salary this job carried, there was the added incentive of a twice yearly production bonus, and if we did particularly well the senior staff and our wives would be treated to a dinner and cabaret show at the Talk of the Town at Christmas. A private room would be taken over for drinks and introductions before the meal. After the meal there would be dancing before and after the cabaret. As far as the job itself went, I was given a pretty free hand in the introduction of new labour saving equipment, and the reorganisation of the book-keeping procedure enabling the factory to become more cost effective and improving on the production figures of my predecessor. Even here, however, I was not completely free from the bigotry of working class colour prejudice.

I once actually had the experience of a member of my staff refusing to carry out my instructions with the rejoinder, 'I am not bloody well doing that, you can do it yourself'. Of course I had no alternative but to give him his marching orders, whereupon he told me point blank that I could not give him the sack without first referring the matter to the West End head office. Well, he did see someone in the West End office after his

103

dismissal, but was given short shrift with the explanation that the factory was not run from the West End, but by the man on the spot who was being very well paid to do just that.

This firm was Jewish, and the three brothers who owned and ran it knew all there was to know about racial prejudice, having been forced to flee Germany shortly after Hitler came to power. Had this been a non-Jewish firm, I cannot help asking myself, would I have had the same backing? On second thoughts, the question is academic as I would never have been given the job in the first place. How sad it is that 38 years after fighting and winning a devastating war to end racial discrimination, black people in Britain are still subject to racial and colour discrimination in jobs and housing, and even our basic civil liberties. What is even worse this treatment is not confined to extremist political bodies, but from the very establishment itself. Everyone must know about the various immigration laws enacted by both Labour and Conservative governments in recent years, aimed, whatever they may say to the contrary, at the black people of this country.

Is it any wonder that certain sections of the police feel they have a mandate to harass and discriminate against the black citizens of their community? Of course not!

In conclusion I would like to say this to the politicians and all racial bigots, 'this is our home, our children's home, and we intend to stay and fight if needs be for our rightful place in the society'. This present visit of mine to Jamaica should have taken place six months earlier, but the demands of the factory made it extremely difficult at the time, so in consideration for my postponing my trip to a later date, I was granted an extra two weeks paid leave, and my forfeited deposit on my passage refunded. So there I was after more than two decades once again on the deck of a ship outside Kingston harbour, viewing the same scene which I did those many years ago, and with the same mixed feelings. How much has my native land changed in those years? But even more to the point, how much have I changed? The answer to these questions must however remain unanswered for the present. My immediate task was to gather my luggage for disembarkation.